Energy and Social Change

Energy and Social Change

James O'Toole and the University
of Southern California Center for
Futures Research

The MIT Press
Cambridge, Massachusetts, and London, England

This book was set in IBM Composer Univers
by Techdata Associates Incorporated, printed
on Fernwood Black and White, and bound in
G.S.B. S/535 82 by The Colonial Press Inc.
in the United States of America.

Library of Congress Cataloging in Publication
Data

O'Toole, James.
  Energy and social change.

  Bibliography: p.
  Includes Index.
    1.Energy policy — United States. 2.United
States— Social conditions — 1960- 3.Eco-
nomic forecasting— United States. I.Los
Angeles. University of Southern California.
Center for Futures Research. II.Title.
HD9502.U5208 333.7 76-44015
ISBN 0-262-15018-2

Contents

Acknowledgments

In 1973, the Center for Futures Research at the University of Southern California initiated a limited experiment to explore the potential of futures methods to contribute meaningful, useful, and imaginative long-range data to top management in the public and private sectors. *Energy and Social Change* is the result of that experiment. The study is based on investigations undertaken by three USC task forces who drew on (1) papers they commissioned; (2) a Delphi inquiry undertaken by Olaf Helmer especially for this study; and (3) the analyses of the task force members themselves based on traditional historical, economic, and systems methods. This report is the synthesis of the task force findings, modified to clarify and rectify several of the inconsistencies and disagreements inevitable when a dozen scholars from diverse backgrounds apply their collective talents to the study of a controversial issue.

I have drawn heavily on the contributions of all my colleagues in the preparation of the study. Several lengthy sections are directly based on drafts by others. Particular credit must be given to the following individuals for their contributions to the sections of chapters indicated in parenthesis: James Calderwood (Chapter 3, "International Effects of Rising Energy Prices"), Selwyn Enzer (passages in Chapter 3 and Chapter 4, "The Advantages of Electricity"), Solomon Golomb (Chapter 4, "Ultimate Abundance?"), Olaf Helmer (Chapter 5), Daniel Kaspar (Chapter 3, "Effects of Alternative Government Policies," Chapter 4, "Innovation and Competition"), John Orr (Chapter 3, "Changing Expectations and Values"), and Hugo Pomrehn (opening section of Chapter 2).

The staff of the Center for Futures Research wishes to acknowledge the efforts of former USC Business School Deans Ted Brannen (for giving the original impetus to this project) and James Stevenson (for providing the support necessary to complete the study). Thanks are given also to Claude E. Elias for his help in planning the project and to the USC members of the Council on the Future for their continuing encouragement of the effort. Several graduate students contributed their talents to the project, including Ahmet Orhun, Richard

Gallup, Richard Mann, Hugo Pomrehn, James Merski, Marsha Mili-
man, and Francis McCullough. Administrative and clerical contributions above and beyond the call of duty were made by Ellen Rudzik
and Julie Shular.

Finally, there would have been no project without the mother's
milk of scholarship, financial contributions. The Center wishes to
thank the ten organizations that comprise the external members of
the USC Council on the Future. These organizations deserve much
credit for providing the wherewithal to undertake this study; however, no responsibility for any of the findings, conclusions, or shortcomings of the study should be attributed to them. Their support
was offered without strings, conditions, or any kind of editorial control. The USC Council on the Future includes representatives from
the following organizations:

Atlantic Richfield Company Foundation

CALTRANS (State of California Department of Transportation)

Ford Motor Company Fund

General Electric Foundation

Pitney Bowes

Sears, Roebuck and Company

Standard Oil of California

Standard Oil (Indiana)

TRW

Union Carbide

Center for Futures Research, Graduate School of Business Administration
James O'Toole
Director, Study of Energy and Social Change

Selwyn Enzer
Director, Study of Impacts of the World Food Supply Problem on American Society

Olaf Helmer
Chairman, USC Council on the Future and Quinton Professor of Futures Research

Burt Nanus
Director, Center for Futures Research

Task Force on Industrial Impacts of Energy
George Hoffman
Asociate Professor of Engineering (Chairman)

Robert Hellwarth
Professor of Physics and Electrical Engineering

Henry Schloss
Professor of Finance and Business Economics

Paul Gray
Associate Professor and Chairman of the Department of Quantitative Business Analysis

Task Force on Social Effects of Energy
John Orr
Director, School of Religion (Chairman)

Malcolm Klein
Professor and Chairman of the Department of Sociology and Anthropology

James Rosenau
Professor of International Relations and Political Science

Daniel Kasper
Assistant Professor of Management

Task Force on Opportunities of Energy Availability
Donald Pyke
Coordinator of Academic Planning for USC (Chairman)

Solomon Golomb
Professor of Electrical Engineering and Mathematics

James Calderwood
Professor of Finance and Business Economics

Jeffrey Chapman
Assistant Professor of Public Administration

Commissioned Papers and Student Papers
William J. Barger
"Will Scarcity of Energy Lead to the Substitution of Labor for Capital?"

Jeffrey Chapman and Hugh Hunter
"The Effects of Energy Availability on Industrial Structure."

Wayne Clark
"Energy Industry Capital Expenditure Forecast."

Morley English
"The Long-Run Price of Energy Will
Be Down."

George A. Hoffman
"The U.S. Fuel Industry in the 21st
Century."

Hugo Pomrehn
"Technological Forecast of Energy
Systems 1970-2020."

Phillip Vincent
"What Are the Likely Effects of
Energy Availability on the Distribution
of Income and Wealth?"

Introduction

During the last three years the nation has become obsessed with a vision of an oil barrel being inexorably drained, eventually leaving us bereft of the energy that drives our civilization. The initial source of this nightmare—the Arab oil embargo—brought into sharp focus a congeries of issues related to energy: economic growth, the quality of life, and international interdependence. In the popular and scholarly analyses that ensued, a doomsday view of the future of these issues came to prevail. Even among those who normally eschew the reflex notion of a crisis, there was a sense of gloom about the future. The operative word was "limits"—limits to resources, limits to growth, limits to the political, technological, and economic options open to society, limits to the ability of the American system to respond to new and complex situations, and most distressingly even limits to the imagination of the human race and its willingness to rescue itself from imminent peril.

In this report we take a step back from this relatively common pessimism and offer at least a modicum of optimism concerning the effects of energy availability on American society. From a perspective not biased by queues of autos at gas stations, we have been able to focus on the long-term energy options and opportunities of the nation, rather than solely on the constraints that limit effective policy response. To be sure, economies, societies, and polities are characterized in great part by the constraints within which they must function—bills must be paid, competing interests must be served, and conflicts must be resolved through compromise. However, it is our feeling that because of recent shocks to the American system (such as the failure of the war on poverty, the Watergate scandal, and the oil embargo), America's political, economic, and intellectual leadership may be overreacting in stressing the limits and weaknesses of the system, while shortchanging its adaptability and strengths. If this report has a contribution to make to the current energy debate, then, it is to suggest a modest redirection of the attention of policy makers to some overlooked but realistic energy options and opportunities that might be realized within the limits of the existing system.

This study identifies two quite separate energy futures for America:
a near term that can be forecasted with some certainty and a long
term that is relatively open and unfixed, a future that still can be
shaped by the decisions made now and in the next few crucial years.

In the near term (between today and 1985 or 1990), we foresee
few severe social or economic dislocations as a result of energy scarcity. Clearly, the price of energy will and should continue to rise.
The rising price will force conservation, substitutions of products,
practices, and processes, and even some considerable sacrifices—but
the price will rise at a pace that is generally gradual and manageable.
At times and for certain industries and individuals, the rising price
may cause financial distress, but in the aggregate the effect will be
neither dramatic nor unbearable. The basic assumption behind this
conclusion is that the importance of energy as a driving force in society has, in recent years, often been overstated or misstated. Although
energy is one particularly important factor in influencing American
life-styles, standards of living, and economic processes and industrial
practices, we are reluctant to identify it as the determining factor.

In the American economy we foresee continued growth (but at a
slower pace than over the last two decades), continued inflation (but
at acceptable levels), falling rates of unemployment, and a slight shift
toward greater economic equality. Capital will very likely be available for new energy developments, but not at the level forecasted as
"needed" by the energy industries (for reasons we outline, these needs
may have been overstated). We foresee less concentration of capital
in the economy, more power accruing to commercial banks, and,
especially, more federal intervention in the energy marketplace—particularly through research and development investments and antitrust activities.

In the international sphere, the OPEC cartel is forecasted to break
up, most likely within the next decade. Another Arab-Israeli war is
highly likely. The probability is that more international cooperation
will go hand-in-hand with increased conflict between the developed

and underdeveloped nations—a seeming contradiction, but its resolution constitutes the greatest diplomatic challenge of coming decades.

Technologically, changes in energy availability probably will not lead to significant new developments within the next decade. Indeed, one of our most important conclusions is that values determine both the choice of technology and the use of energy to a greater degree than technology and energy determine the way humans think, act, and live. Technologically, the most portentous possibility we find is that America may well be reaching the point of diminishing returns in terms of additional energy inputs in the production of goods and services. If true, this means that future material progress will not ensue from greater industrial investment in energy use as it has in the past. The consequences of this finding have profound implications— but not for the coming decade.

In the social context startling changes in life-styles and living behavior patterns are highly improbable. As a result of energy scarcity we foresee scant possibility of a significant short-term middle-class resettlement of the central cities, switch from the use of private cars to public transportation, or substitution of telecommunications for transportation. In the future, Americans will probably live much as they do today—doing the same sorts of things, living in the same kinds of places, driving cars quite similar to contemporary models, and using electricity to make the most onerous tasks more pleasant. Some conservation will, of course, occur as the result of higher energy prices—there is likely to be less joyriding, more car pooling, and more walking. Buildings and houses may be cooler in the winter and hotter in the summer. Autos will be somewhat smaller, lighter, and slower. But these adjustments will be gradual, and apparently not of an order of magnitude greatly different from those made in America in the recent past. If human values change radically, most likely the shift will be in the direction of more individual responses to social problems and toward a decline in social and economic expectations about the future.

Because such fossil fuels as petroleum (and to a lesser extent natural gas) will still be available during the next decade, few severe social or economic dislocations are likely. Higher prices will force conservation, substitution, and some sacrifice, but this process will be gradual and manageable though at times a bit unpleasant and hard on the pocketbook.

What is crucial is not what will actually happen during the period 1976 to 1985 as the consequence of higher energy prices, but what will happen in the subsequent decades as the result of choices made during this time. Beginning in about 1990 to 2000, little can be forecasted with certainty. The future, either one of scarcity or one of abundance, depends on the choices being made now and over the next ten years.

The Long-Term Future

In these pages, we argue that it is possible to create a quality economy in the long-term future—an economy characterized by a reduction of waste, of inefficiency, and of pollution, by more meaningful and plentiful jobs, and by goods that contribute to a high quality of life. Whether the nation achieves this quality economy or inherits an economy of scarcity hinges on how effectively decision makers in the public and private sectors make substitutions for scarce forms of energy.

The rising price of energy will by itself force substitution and change in the American economy. Choices will still have to be made. Higher prices do not eliminate the need to plan; rather, they heighten the requirement to understand the long-term consequences of the options open to decision makers. For example, higher energy prices open up five aggregate alternatives:

- Substituting energy for energy—an abundant resource like coal for a scarce one like natural gas.

- Substituting capital for energy—adopting a new, more energy-efficient technology.

- Substituting a product for energy—making a dress out of cotton rather than nylon or making liquid detergents rather than powdered detergents.

- Substituting processes for energy—installing windows that open in office buildings.

- Substituting labor for energy—assembling a radio by hand instead of mechanically.

Which of these substitutions to make will depend on the industry in question and on the analysis of the second- and third-order consequences of the alternatives. Businessmen, economists, and engineers tend to favor the first two options because these are consistent with the traditional concepts of economic efficiency. However, changes in values, new environmental concerns, and notions of corporate social responsibility may force future-oriented executives to weigh also the costs and benefits of the latter three forms of substitutions.

In such deliberations, choosing technologies appropriate to the future will be important too. For reasons of energy and capital efficiency, productivity, and worker satisfaction, it will probably be necessary for future executives to choose processes that move toward the ends of the technological continuum as opposed to the middle-range technologies that were developed in the later part of the industrial era.

The Technological Continuum

	Low Technology	Middle Technology	High Technology
	←	Trend	→
1. Energy efficiency	Very high	Low	Medium
2. Capital use efficiency	High	Medium	Very high
3. Productivity	Medium/low	Medium	Very high
4. Quality of goods	High	Low	High
5. Environmental soundness	High	Low	Medium
6. Worker satisfaction	Very high	Low	High
7. Labor intensity	Very high	Medium/low	Medium/high

   In the middle range of the continuum are the mass-production
technologies that characterize the late industrial era. The challenge is
to replace the industrial activities in the center of the continuum
with those technologies nearer the poles in which energy, capital,
and labor are used more efficiently, in which the environment is less
adversely affected, and in which the quality of goods and jobs is
highest. The traditional task of managers of choosing the right technologies and the right production mix is thus more important than
ever before—but the factors influencing their decisions are concomitantly more complex and the consequences of their options less clear.

Technological Alternatives
Some desirable technological alternatives, however, are becoming distinct and salient. For example, a shift to a more electrically based
economy would offer the nation much needed flexibility in the tur-
bulent decades ahead and help to concentrate the effects of pollution. Moreover, increased research effort should probably be invested
in creating a superbattery that would make advanced and clean energy sources such as solar and wind power more attractive.
   One of the most remarkable forecasts made by the Delphi panel
was the 50 percent probability of development of superbatteries in
the next fifteen years and 90 percent probability within twenty
years. Should a breakthrough in portable electrical-energy storage
devices occur, it would revolutionize the energy and transportation
situation in America. Such a development would initially be used in
electrically propelled cars, buses, and trucks. This would permit a
greater shift in basic fuels from petroleum and gas to coal and nuclear power. It would also change the cost trade-off associated with
solar energy systems, because the batteries would permit decentralized solar energy to be used and stored so that they not only provided light and heat during the night hours, but also provided energy
for personal transportation vehicles. The price of petroleum would
drop on the world market and the concern over its depletion would
dwindle considerably. Petroleum would be used in very few applica-

tions—primarily in the petrochemical areas and for such specialized purposes as aircraft fuel. The environmental impact of such a breakthrough would be immense. Most air pollution problems would disappear.

The battery is only one of the many promising responses to the energy question. Why is it that these innovative alternatives are not being pursued with the vigor associated with, say, fusion research? In the study several reasons for the lack of innovation are identified, including disincentives to entrepreneurial activity in many large corporations and the bureaucratic effect of some government controls that stifle potentially efficient and effective market responses to national problems. What might be done in the public and private sectors to meet the challenge of the energy issue?

Alternative Public Policies and Private Practices

The method of analysis used in the study is illustrated by the accompanying relevance tree, which indicates that America can obtain an adequate energy supply by 1995 through pursuing two basic courses: increasing the supply of petroleum and gas and reducing demand for petroleum and gas. We find that it will be necessary to pursue both policies simultaneously. To do so successfully will require a strong federal commitment to four policies: (1) higher energy prices; (2) incentives to make the domestic energy market more competitive (which would include such steps as deregulation of the price of natural gas); (3) greater incentives for exploration and conservation (including a more rational arrangement for leasing offshore fields and economic incentives for companies that install energy-saving and nonpolluting technologies); and (4) programs that help offset the effects of higher energy prices on the poorest families.

Because the effects of energy availability will vary from business to business it is not possible to present a comprehensive list of the implications of the study for corporate planners. However, the following kinds of general implications seem to emerge from the analysis:

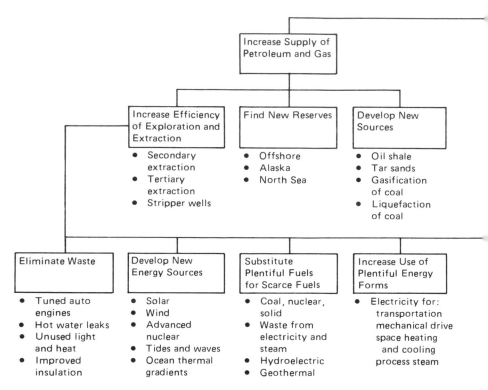

Relevance Tree Showing Alternative Means of Providing an Adequate Energy Supply by 1995

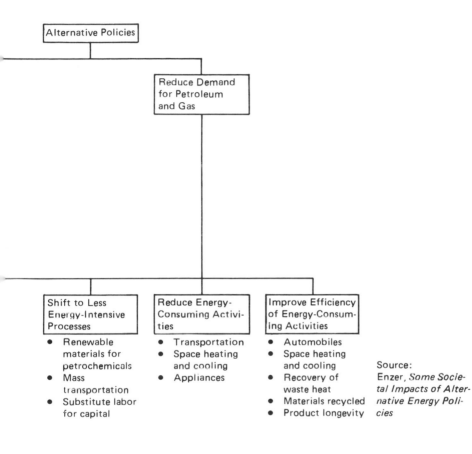

Source:
Enzer, *Some Socie-*
tal Impacts of Alter-
native Energy Poli-
cies

Alternative Policies

Reduce Demand
for Petroleum
and Gas

Shift to Less
Energy-Intensive
Processes
- Renewable
  materials for
  petrochemicals
- Mass
  transportation
- Substitute labor
  for capital

Reduce Energy-
Consuming Activi-
ties
- Transportation
- Space heating
  and cooling
- Appliances

Improve Efficiency
of Energy-Consum-
ing Activities
- Automobiles
- Space heating
  and cooling
- Recovery of
  waste heat
- Materials recycled
- Product longevity

- The energy situation will not change the basic ground rules for U.S. industry, but it will require more careful and complex corporate planning, trend monitoring, policy analysis, and decision-making techniques, particularly in the next decade.

- Because energy research and capital investment will increase disproportionately, this creates an opportunity for those who are prepared to capture these resources, and a problem for those in nonenergy fields who may find such funds less available.

- New capital investments that are expected to produce a return over the next ten to thirty years will require a new planning calculus: Plant and equipment in the future will need to be not only energy-efficient, but energy-flexible (that is, capable of using a variety of fuels).

- Because large, concentrated industries in mass-production fields will be the most seriously affected by energy dislocations as well as capital shortages, diversification for these industries should be toward products at either end of the technological continuum.

- As capital, energy, and other natural resources become relatively more scarce in the future, the development and proper utilization of human resources will become the prime task of management.

Ultimate Abundance?
In the very long run, there is good reason for optimism about the supply of energy. In the midst of the energy crisis of 1973-1974 it was easy to slip into pessimism by forgetting that the world economy ultimately operates on the laws of supply and demand. Eventually increases in the price of a commodity bring a host of restoring forces into play. The recent increase in the price of crude oil was so dramatic that the restoring forces generated may not be felt for a decade —but they will be felt.

It may take several years for a country like the United States to make the transition from passenger automobiles that average 10 miles per gallon to those averaging 35 miles per gallon, but such a transition is clearly under way. And in any one of at least a dozen technological areas, a breakthrough could occur at almost any time that would have the effect of significantly increasing the quantity of energy available relative to human needs.

No doubt, ultimate abundance is still an iffy proposition. But the factors most likely to turn *if* into *when* are high energy prices brought about by market pressures and the unconstrained imagination of American entrepreneurs. The factor most likely to lead to ultimate scarcity is short-run complacency brought about by temporary relaxations by the Organization of Petroleum Exporting Countries (OPEC) cartel on oil price increases. Alarmingly, in mid-1976, Americans were again purchasing gas-guzzling cars in great numbers, industry was slipping back into wasteful practices, and the government was beginning to soften its proposals for energy conservation and production.

In brief, the purpose of this report is not to retrace the ground covered by many others in recent years. Rather, we concentrate on identifying policies needed to help offset the short-run disbenefits of higher energy prices and on policies needed to develop abundant energy and continued improvement in the quality of life in the long-term future.

1. The Past: Historical Perspectives

If, then, you ask me to put into one sentence the cause of . . . recent, rapid, and enormous change, and the prognosis for the achievement of human liberty, I should reply, It is found in the discovery and utilization of the means by which heat energy can be made to do man's work for him.

Robert Millikan (1940)
Nobel Prize Winner, Physics

The Arab oil embargo of 1973 and subsequent increases in the price of petroleum products have focused public attention on America's dependence on energy. Even beyond this so-called energy crisis, experts now warn of impending shortages not only of petroleum but of all natural resources. Representative of the thinking of this now popular neo-Malthusian gloom and doom school are Ehrlich's *The End of Affluence*, Watt's *The Titanic Effect*, Meadows's *Limits to Growth*, Daly's *Toward a Steady State Economy*, Melman's *Our Depleted Society*, and the Ford Foundation's *A Time to Choose*.

The common theme of these books is compelling: the world's supply of natural resources is finite; the exponential extrapolation of trends in resource consumption shows the world running out of resources in the next century; therefore, we must conserve or face extinction. These authors marshall considerable evidence to show that, indeed, there are physical limits to growth.

How might decision makers and concerned citizens evaluate these pessimistic forecasts? Because the future does not yet exist, it is rather difficult to assess objectively whether energy and other resource shortages will lead the world to imminent doom as the experts predict.

One way of evaluating future forecasts is to look at historical precedents to gain at least some perspective—no matter how flawed the past might be as a mirror of the future. The first thing evident when reviewing the historical data is that in isolation energy has had little effect on social change. The discovery of fire without doubt raised man an additional notch above the apes, and the use of the sun's rays to nourish crops clearly was and is essential for life, but it has only

been when man has used technology to harness energy that significant social change has occurred.

The use of the hoe to increase the efficiency of the first farmers
and the later use of the ox before the plough to increase man's puny
muscle power geometrically were prerequisites of the most profound
of all social changes: the transformation of human society from
nomadic bands of hunters and gatherers to settled communities of
cultivators of crops and domesticators of animals. Once settled at the
fork of some African or Asian river, early man began his ascent to
civilization. Eventually, however, he discovered that he needed more
than animal energy. He then built a waterwheel. But the shallow,
slow-moving river could not for long match his rising expectations of
the power he needed. At some time lost to history, he then built a
dam on the river. This process—higher energy needs → new technology → even higher energy needs—has been escalating ever since.

Thus, the first perspective gained from history is that *energy is
scarce or abundant only relative to available technologies*, which is a
rather basic point unfortunately overlooked in the *Limits to Growth*
and other recent energy studies.

History is similarly instructive on other fronts. A second perspective well worth consideration is that *a minor technological breakthrough can have profound social and political implications.* Medieval
historian Lynn White has provided the quintessential documentation
of this point.[1] In the sixth century Northwestern Europe was little
more than a battleground for constantly warring tribes over whom
no one political power could exert hegemony. It was not until the
reigns of Carolingians—Martel, Carloman, and Pepin—that political
order under a strong central monarchy was established. Remarkably,
the device that facilitated the establishment of a feudal system in
France was the simple stirrup. Until the Carolingians introduced the
stirrup, warfare in Europe had been conducted by bands of men running around the countryside wielding swords and axes or shooting
arrows—a rather inefficient way to bring about political order. What
was needed was a kind of medieval tank—the armed knight on horse-

back. But without a stirrup, a heavily armed knight with both hands on a broadsword could be knocked off a horse by even a mild gust of wind. In such a precarious position, fighting was simply out of the question. If both hands were not on the reins, the knight had to hold himself on the steed with his feet. With the introduction of the simple stirrup, the Carolingians came to be served by an efficient fighting machine. Martel then reorganized his realm along feudal lines to make it possible to support great numbers of mounted fighters. He seized church lands and distributed them to his vassals on condition that they served him, their liege, as knights. According to White, the duty of knight's service thus became the touchstone of feudalism.

The knights needed land as a kind of logistical lifeline to support their chivalrous duties. They needed land to raise and feed their many horses, to support a retinue of retainers, and the wealth it created to provide the leisure time for a warrior's lengthy apprenticeship.

White writes that change in the number and mix of people engaged in a basic endeavor (such as agriculture, war, factory work) modifies the whole of society: population, wealth, political relationships, leisure and cultural expression. In sum, it is White's thesis that in medieval France the introduction of a simple technological device, the stirrup, created

a new form of Western European society dominated by an aristocracy of warriors endowed with land so they might fight in a new and highly specialized way. Inevitably this nobility developed cultural forms and patterns of thought and emotion in harmony with its style of mounted shock combat and its social posture; as Denholm Young has said: "It is impossible to be chivalrous without a horse."[2]

The introduction of the heavy plough in Northern Europe several centuries later had an impact on society as great as that of the stirrup. This rather sophisticated plough opened up the richest lands for cultivation and made possible the surplus food needed for population growth, urbanization, specialization, and the growth of leisure.[3] Eventually it created the necessary conditions for the germination of petty capitalism. Significantly, the plough needed eight oxen to pull it through the rain-heavy soil of Germany and other northern countries. This led to a cooperative manorial economy in Northern Europe as opposed to the individualistic economy that developed in Southern Europe where one ox could pull the plough through the dry sun-baked soil. White cites other examples of technology influencing social change: In the seventeenth and eighteenth centuries, Turnip Townshend and other agronomists developed root and fodder crops that produced surplus food that freed additional labor from the fields for work in the factories of the industrial revolution.[4]

It might seem from this evidence that human history is determined by technological change—that once a breakthrough is made, man will inevitably adopt it and, in the process, have his society changed by it. Not so, says White. This is a third important perspective to be gained from history: *man is free to choose among available technologies and free to use them in different ways.* The stirrup, for example, had been known for centuries and in many different cultures, but for some complex reason it was the Carolingians who adopted it in Europe and it was they who saw its warfare and political potential. White explains that

As our understanding of the history of technology increases, it becomes clear that a new device merely opens a door, it does not compel one to enter. The acceptance or rejection of an invention, or the extent to which its implications are realized if it is accepted, depends quite as much upon the conditions of a society, and upon the imagination of its leaders, as upon the nature of the technological item itself.[5]

White's historical interpretations cast the "inevitability" of some of the more pessimistic future forecasts into considerable doubt.

Another significant perspective to be gained from history is that *transitions from one form of energy to another—even those involving the depletion of a major source of energy—are not necessarily fraught with disaster.* For example, during the twelfth and thirteenth centuries, men became frustrated by the constraints of animal power and began in earnest to attempt to harness natural forces to provide energy. They used windmills, water mills, treadmills, gravity, magnetism, and mechanical devices such as the cam, the crank, and the flywheel. They even developed a one-cylinder internal combustion engine—the cannon. (White argues that their success is attested to by the ruling of Pope Celestine III in the 1190s that windmills must pay tithes.)[6] Medieval man even searched for a perpetual motion machine—with obvious parallels to our own almost alchemistic hopes for fission breeders and fusion reactors. In 1260, Roger Bacon forecast that

Machines may be made by which the largest ships, with only one man steering them, will be moved faster than if they were filled with rowers; wagons may be built which will move with incredible speed and without the aid of beasts; flying machines can be constructed in which a man . . . may beat the air with wings like a bird . . . machines will make it possible to go to the bottom of seas and rivers.[7]

Through a combination of futuristic dreaming and practical engineering, man has historically been able to use technology to meet his energy needs—which are really escalating wants or desires. However, from time to time there have been dislocations in the process. In the sixteenth century, the price of hardwood for fuel dramatically increased throughout Europe, because the demand for fuel was increasing at the same time as alternative use of hardwood for ship construction and furniture was on the rise.[8] The response to this early energy crisis was the development of technology to use coal as a replacement for wood as a basic energy source. Significantly, this change required new inventions to be able to smelt iron using coal rather than wood as the fuel. At the time these innovations may not have seemed important, but they laid the technological groundwork for the coming industrial revolution—an enormous transformation that could not have been fueled on wood.

In the last century, another energy crisis occurred when the whale oil needed to light the lamps of America grew increasingly scarce. Although there may have been some panic at the time, it has been forgotten now. What is recalled is the resourceful way in which Americans began to exploit their previously neglected reserves of petroleum.[9]

The last historical perspective offered here is that *although changes in the availability of a particular form of energy do not necessitate crises, they often do portend significant social change.* For example, the population of Britain had remained at a more or less steady 11 million for many decades before Watt invented the steam engine. Once the steam engine was powering the industrial revolution, Britain experienced a concomitant population explosion.[10] More dramatically, the rather peaceful switch from whale oil to petroleum in the United States led to an era of unprecedented prosperity and mobility for the nation—and to freeways, urban sprawl, pollution, and the often noted fact that Americans were then able to be sired, born, raised, and die in Detroit's contribution to Western civilization.

In summary history tells us that energy does affect social change—if not as simply or as predictably as some commentators have assumed, yet perhaps more positively and more controllably.

The Future as History

Interestingly, futures forecasters use many of the same methods as historians for analyzing questions of social change.[11] Futures forecasting is often criticized as being unscientific or unreliable because it is based on such scanty evidence that each futurist arrives at his own unique vision of the future. But as Karl Popper points out, historians are in the same boat: "There is no history of mankind, there is only an indefinite number of histories of all kinds of aspects of human life."[12] There are as many views of history as there are historians. The cause of the decline and fall of Rome has been proved

by historians to have been the result of everything from lead poison-
ing to buggery—and there is no sign of consensus on cause (or even
that Rome fell) even though historians are all presumably dealing
with the same facts. As futurist David MacMichael writes

history is not the record of what happened but is the process of
thinking about what happened. There can be as many histories as
there are thinkers. . . . Basically, anyone is entitled to review the evidence, to introduce new evidence, and come to new or different conclusions about the meaning of a past event. . . . It can be argued that
the historical process is a means for the production of alternative
pasts.[13]

But it is often objected that there are no data about the future. We
might respond that there are little or no data about Paleolithic man,
either. Yet working with little more than a fragment of a jawbone,
archaeologists nevertheless "scientifically" recreate his way of life.
For certain periods of classical Rome all that remains are a couple of
diaries and an official document or two, yet historians have documented an entire era on such evidence.

The argument is not that we know as much about the future as we
know about the past. Rather, we probably know less about the past
than we often assume, and we have better information about the
future than we have been willing to admit. In some respects, there are
considerable data about the future, as MacMichael demonstrates:
demographic data can in some cases be reliably projected as far as
fifty years into the future. Capital investments, too, are unlikely to
change—machines, factories, buildings will not be destroyed until
they have been depreciated. Existing freeways, railroads, bridges, and
canals are likely still to be in place twenty years from now. Trust
funds, retirement funds, and other investments are not terribly liquid.
Military and other capital construction schedules and plans often extend ten to fifteen years. And some scheduled events—such as elec-
tions and conventions—have a high probability of occurring.[14]

The secret of good futures forecasting is the same as the secret of good historical analysis: using one's data imaginatively and well.

Summary

Before examining the current data available about the future of energy and social change, let us quickly review our history lessons:

- Energy is scarce or abundant only relative to available technologies.

- A minor technological breakthrough can have profound social and political implications.

- Societies are free to choose among available technologies and free to use them in different ways. Society is not determined by available technologies.

- Transitions from one form of energy to another—even those involving the depletion of a major source of energy—are not necessarily fraught with disaster.

- Although changes in the availability of a particular form of energy do not necessitate crisis, they often do portend significant social change.

What have these historical lessons taught us about the future? Is the current energy situation parallel to the historical transition from hardwoods to coal, or the substitution of petroleum for whale oil? Is there a "stirrup" in our future? In response, these lessons anticipate the argument that follows in this report: in the short run, changes in energy availability will not lead to significant new technologies; hence the effects on society will not be revolutionary. In the long run, new technologies will be required, and these technologies (which turn out to be surprisingly undramatic) may transform Western economies and societies. But significantly it is not at all a sure thing that people in these societies will choose to adopt the relatively simple technological changes required to transform for the better the quality of their lives.

**The trouble with our time is
that the future is not what it
used to be.**   Paul Valéry

There are two basic forms of energy resources: income forms that are
produced continuously in nature and are thus considered readily replenishable reservoirs, and capital forms that have accumulated over
aeons of time and are not readily replenishable when they are ex-
hausted.
Income energy resource forms include

- Solar radiation
- Hydro power
- Ocean thermal gradients
- Wind power

- Tidal energy
- Animal power
- Photochemical energy in plants and animals

Capital energy resource forms include

- Fossil hydrocarbons
  Oil (petroleum, shale, tar sands)
  Coal
  Natural gas

- Nuclear
  Uranium-235
  Uranium-238
  Thorium-232
  Lithium-6

Modern industrial societies are characterized by an enormous consumption of energy at the expense of capital rather than income energy forms. As Exhibit 1 shows, this trend is fairly recent. Only in the
last hundred years or so has man changed his emphasis from income
forms to capital forms of energy. The advanced industrial societies
are further characterized by their increasing dependence on electricity, a trend that has direct effects on the growth of energy consumption and indirect effects on environmental quality. Electricity generation in North America has grown at the rate of 7 percent between
1963 and 1971.[1]
Quantum leaps in the growth of energy consumption have accom-

panied movements to higher stages of human development (Exhibits 2 and 3). About a million years ago, primitive man in East Africa, without the use of fire, used only the energy of the food he ate, or about 2,000 kilocalories per day. Hunting man in Europe about a hundred thousand years ago had more food and also burned wood for heat and cooking. His daily per capita consumption was about 4,000 to 5,000 kilocalories. Primitive agricultural man from the fertile crescent in 5000 B.C. was growing crops and harnessing animal energy, and thus utilized about 12,000 kilocalories per day. Advanced agricultural man of Northern Europe in 1400 A.D. had some coal for heating, some water and wind power, and animal transport. His daily per capita consumption ran to 20,000 to 30,000 kilocalories. Industrial man had the steam engine at the height of the so-called low-technology industrial revolution (from approximately 1850 to 1870), so that per capita daily consumption reached 70,000 kilocalories in England, Germany, and the United States.[2] A succeeding high-technology revolution (brought about by central-station electric power and the automobile) enabled the average person to acquire power in his home and on the road. Beginning shortly before the 1900s, per capita energy consumption in the United States rose at an increasing rate to the 1970 figure of about 230,000 kilocalories per day (or its equivalent 65×10^{15} [65q] BTU per year).[3] The per capita growth in energy demand in the United States and the world since the 1800s is shown in Exhibit 4 with extrapolations into the next century.[4]

Exhibit 3 also illustrates world population over time. Population growth seems to have taken place in three surges as a result of the cultural (hunting, clothing, and fire), agricultural, and technological revolutions. Each of these surges reflects a great increase in man's control of energy. After each of the first two revolutions, population leveled off as resource limits were approached. As the technology of hunting became more sophisticated and efficient, the number of wild animals started to decline. In fact, several species became extinct. As primitive agriculture spread throughout the accessible arable world, the older soil became depleted and eroded and the marginal areas lim-

Exhibit 1
Man's Use of Energy through the Millennia

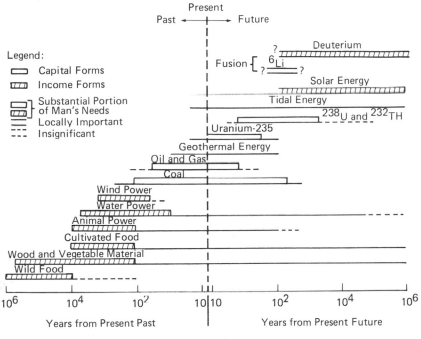

Source: Cook, "Energy Sources for the Future"

Exhibit 2
Daily Consumption of Energy per Capita for Six Stages In Human Development

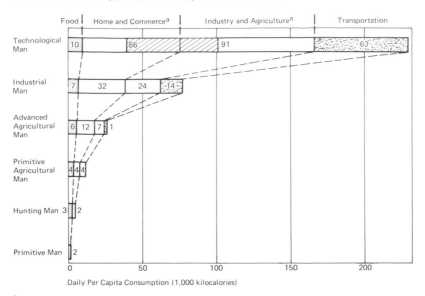

Daily Per Capita Consumption (1,000 kilocalories)

[a]The hatched area indicates the portion of energy needs fulfilled by electricity.

Source: Cook, "The Flow of Energy in an Industrial Society"

Exhibit 3
Population and Per Capita Daily Consumption of Energy, 1,000,000 B.C. to 2000 A.D.

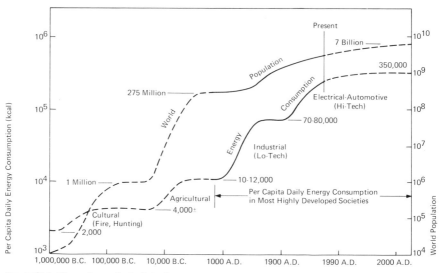

Source: Cook, "Energy Sources for the Future"

Exhibit 4
Growth in Per Capita Energy Demand

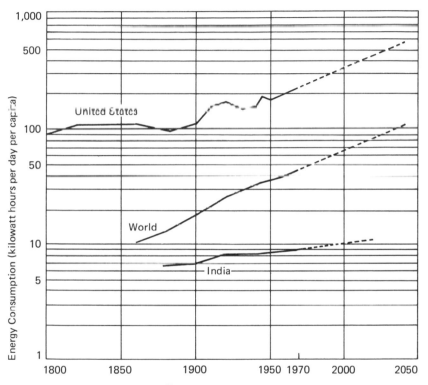

Source: Starr, "Energy and Power"

ited expansion. Because of this, world population in the first seven
hundred years of the Christian era may have actually declined.[5] Sub-
sequently, the technological revolution led to a surge of population
growth nourished by the vast energy resources technological man has
been able to develop. Because each of these three revolutions brought
man to a higher level of per capita consumption of energy, man's
total energy use has increased even faster than has population. The
apparent dip in per capita energy consumption in the late nineteenth
century shown in Exhibit 4 can be explained by the great increase in
efficiency of energy used during the so-called low-technology era.

In the United States, total primary energy consumption has grown
at the rate of about 3 percent annually since 1850, although the rate
has increased to over 4 percent during the past 10 years.[6] In 1850,
90 percent of this energy was supplied by renewable sources—wood,
water, and wind power. Currently, more than 75 percent is supplied
by hydrocarbon fuels, petroleum, and natural gas.[7] World energy
consumption in the same period grew at a similar rate. Since 1950,
however, world consumption has grown at the rate of better than 5
percent.[8]

Not all people in the world participated in the technological revolution. Exhibit 4 shows that worldwide energy consumption per capita
increased about 400 percent in the last century, but is still only about
one fifth of the U.S. average. In fact, much less than half of the
world's population has as yet experienced the technological revolution. The split between the energy haves and the have-nots began in
about the seventh century A.D. The differences were hardly percepti-
ble at that time, but by the late Middle Ages living standards in North-
west Europe were appreciably better than those in Asia and Africa,
and by the nineteenth century the contrasts were enormous. This
wide average income gap between the developed and the less-developed countries is caused primarily by a nontechnological culture and
tradition in the less-developed countries and their lack of the capital
necessary for industrialization. Further, modern medicine and sanita-
tion have dramatically lowered mortality rates in the less-developed

countries and, arguably, may even have increased population beyond
supportable limits.

Economic Growth and Energy Consumption

The economic growth of nations has been strongly correlated with increases in the use of energy. Indeed, when per capita energy consumption and per capita GNP are plotted against each other (Exhibit 5) the
resulting points fall within a fairly narrow band. However, the demand for energy for a given nation is related not only to the form of
its economy, but also to its population, its culture, its relative emphasis on industry or on services, and on its relative efficiency in converting energy to useful work. Thus the relationship between increased standard of living and energy consumption is not fully understood.[9]

  Exhibit 5 shows that a number of developed countries use more
energy per unit of GNP than the United States, as well as that a number of countries use less. Generally, it can be seen that an increase in
energy use per capita corresponds to an increase in per capita GNP—
although this trend is not necessarily proportional. For example, Luxembourg (which produces a great deal of steel) and Norway (which
produces large quantities of aluminum) do not seem to achieve com-
mensurate economic rewards for very large energy expenditures.
Japan, Sweden, West Germany, and Switzerland maintain fairly high
standards of living with substantially less energy use than the United
States. Statistics for 1972 revealed that Switzerland's per capita GNP
was about that of the United States, using only about half as much
energy per unit of GNP (Exhibit 6).

  This variance in the energy-GNP ratios may be accounted for by
several factors:

- At given income levels a cold country will burn more fuel for residential and other heating and, hence, consume more primary energy than
  a country with a more moderate climate.

- The efficiency with which primary energy forms are used or con-

Exhibit 5
Relationship between GNP and Energy Consumption per Capita for 52 Countries—1971 Data

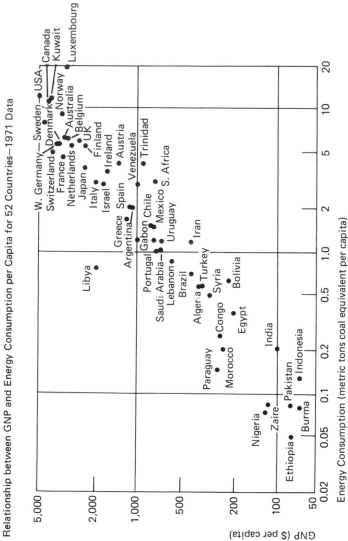

Source: Linden, "Energy Self-Sufficiency"

Exhibit 6
Trend of Energy Consumption per Unit of GNP in Selected Countries

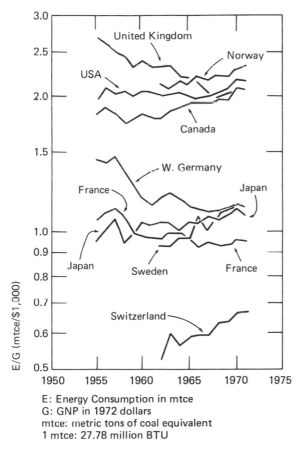

E: Energy Consumption in mtce
G: GNP in 1972 dollars
mtce: metric tons of coal equivalent
1 mtce: 27.78 million BTU

Source: Linden, "Energy Self-Sufficiency"

verted also plays a role. A very high level of energy consumption may, in part, reflect a pronounced thermal inefficiency in electric genera- tion. These inefficiencies stem from the fact that utilities in such countries as Czechoslovakia rely heavily on lignite coal, a fuel with poor combustion properties.

- The industrial structure of a country can explain major differences in energy-GNP ratios. The energy requirements of different industries vary enormously. Thus, when a country's industry mix is dominated by activities with heavy energy content per unit output (such as min- ing, metals, chemicals, or petroleum refining), energy per unit of national output is apt to be relatively high.

Does the United States use energy in an efficient manner? This is the central and as yet unresolvable question of the energy situation. Using published data, we have found it is possible to construct a case that America's energy efficiency ratios have been falling off dramat- ically in the last few years. Simply put, it is possible to show that America is starting to expend more and more energy in industrial processes while getting relatively less and less out in terms of goods produced. However, using the most conservative government figures, it can also be shown that the energy efficiency of American industry has not dropped significantly—even after the energy crisis.[10]

This contradictory evidence cannot be resolved until the govern- ment releases data for the last four years that cover value added in in- dustry and until other inconsistencies in government data are recon- ciled. It is hoped that economists will soon make some sense out of these conflicting data. In the meantime, we have chosen to analyze a set of data that is far from a perfect measure of the nation's energy efficiency but is at least internally consistent: apparently, the ratio of dollars of GNP earned to BTUs of energy consumed peaked in 1965 and has not regained its steady and uninterrupted rise from 1920 (see Exhibit 7).

If these data have any meaning, they could indicate that in the aggregate the United States may be reaching the point of diminishing

Exhibit 7
Ratio of GNP to Energy Consumed, United States, 1920 to 1975

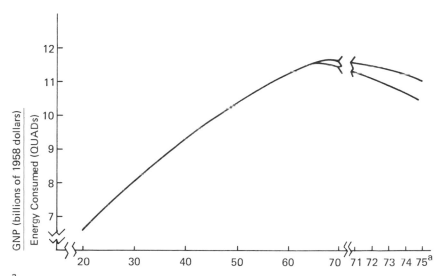

[a]Actual data through 1974. GNP through third quarter, 1975, adjusted to annual figures on seasonal basis. Although energy consumed dropped in 1974, it is expected to start to rise again. Therefore, the precise values are in doubt but the future trend is generally down.

Source: GNP (in billions of 1958 constant dollars) is taken from the *Survey of Current Business* and its biennial supplements, U.S. Department of Commerce. Total energy in QUADs is taken from *Energy Perspectives*, February 1975, U.S. Department of Interior.

returns in terms of additional energy investments in the production
of goods and services.[11]

This does not mean that all the U.S. economy is reaching the point
of diminishing marginal productivity. It does indicate that with higher
energy prices many key industries are likely to become less energy-
productive in the future.

If this trend holds up, it could constitute the makings of a real
energy crisis over the next several decades, a crisis with profound
long-term effects on the society and economy. Significantly, the ratio
of the real dollar value of durable goods produced per million BTUs
also has fallen dramatically since the rise in energy prices in 1973,
giving additional reason to believe that a change is occurring in the
marginal productivity of industrial energy-use patterns. We should
not extrapolate from a small blip in a long curve, but several logical
reasons can be advanced to support the case of diminishing energy
productivity in American industry. It is worth reviewing this evidence
because, if the trend holds up, the end result of greater use of energy
in industrial processes would not be a higher material standard of living but a lower quality of life as the result of growing inflation,
waste, and pollution.

Energy to Burn
In recent years, the effects of unplanned energy policies of the U.S.
government have been to keep the price of energy low. For example,
as the result of price controls, tax incentives, depletion allowances,
and other governmental tools, the relative price of oil dropped by
about 25 percent during the period from 1948 to 1972.[12] Moreover,
as Edward Mitchell has calculated, the relative price of all energy fell
steadily between 1950 and 1973 (Exhibit 8).[13] It is not unusual that
no one complained about the low price of energy during this period—
in the short run everyone was benefiting. Americans are now starting
to suffer the consequences of thirty years of unplanned government
activities in the energy marketplace.

Because the price of energy was so low for so long, many decision

Exhibit 8
The Price of Energy, 1950 to June 1974

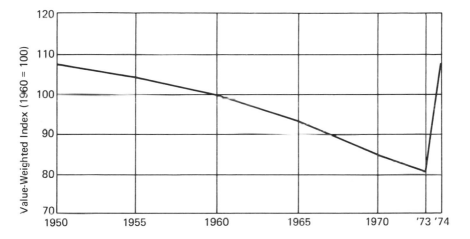

Source: Mitchell, *U.S. Energy Policy: A Primer*

makers involved in designing the appropriate production methods to meet the demands for consumer goods had come to think of energy as a free good. It is remarkable in hindsight that practical business-men, economists, and industrial engineers who lived by the motto "there is no such thing as a free lunch" assumed for decades that such things as air, water, and energy were free. The effects of this mis-conception are being painfully rebalanced now through higher energy costs and strict environmental regulation. Bills long left to run up have now become due. We are now paying a high price for the cheap energy of the past.

The objection to this line of reasoning is that the OPEC cartel price does not represent the real costs of oil. It is absurd to say that oil has been too cheap in the past when the cost of its extraction in the Mid-east is, after all, less than $1 per barrel. How then can a price of $11 per barrel be explained as anything but piracy? As politically com-fortable as such moral indignation may be, there is an economic ex-planation—if not justification—for the current high price of oil and for the argument that it was really too cheap during the last two decades.

In the short run, the price for monopoly commodities in limited supply in nature is determined not only by the costs of production (although this is a contributing factor) but more important by the relative costs of substitutes for the commodity. Although economists lump these and other factors together under the heading of supply and demand, it is nevertheless helpful to disaggregate the analysis to understand the important role of substitutes in pricing. Why is it that water is not terribly expensive? There are, after all, no substitutes for water. The answer is that water is in relatively limitless supply (ex-cept on deserts, where water is expensive because the supply is lim-ited and there are no substitutes). Why is it that the bauxite cartel cannot successfully quadruple the price of their commodity (as OPEC did with oil)? In part, the bauxite cartel is handicapped by the fact that there are competitive substitutes for aluminum (such as steel, magnesium, glass, or cement) for most applications. If it raises its

prices, potential customers will simply seek to substitute a competi-
tively priced commodity. There is a clear limit to the amount of oil
under the earth's surface; thus, it is more like bauxite than water.
More important, possible substitutes are not only relatively expensive
but are either in limited supply (natural gas or methane) or in incon-
venient forms (electricity from coal or nuclear power). Hence it is not
possible to make an easy or inexpensive substitution for oil—especially for use in one's car. In this way, then, a barrel priced at $1 (or
even $10) can be said to be "too cheap." As E.F. Schumacher writes

There are still people who say that if oil prices rose too much (whatever that may mean), oil would price itself out of the market; but it
is perfectly obvious that there is no ready substitute for oil to take
its place on a quantitatively significant scale, so that oil, in fact, cannot price itself out of the market.[14]

Perhaps the worst consequence of the government's activities that
kept the price of energy low was that it nurtured the attitude that we
have energy to burn. Capital investments were made that were prodi-
gal users of energy, and now suddenly the cost of running some
machines and undertaking some industrial processes has multiplied—
particularly in the production of primary metals, chemicals, petroleum, cement and paper, which utilize 50 percent of the industrial
energy in America and 16 percent of the country's total energy. We
are now finding that the construction of homes, offices, and factories
was predicated on the false assumption that energy was always going
to be cheap. For example, constructing buildings with windows that
do not open was always a questionable practice from the viewpoint
of comfort, safety, and environmental degradation—but it was economically justified because the cost of air conditioning was low while
the cost of labor and movable window fixtures was high. Now, building owners and tenants are caught in a squeeze—the cost of air conditioning has soared past the point where it is economically viable to

cool buildings on temperate days, but the buildings are so designed
that fixed windows cannot be replaced by ones that open. From
large gas-guzzling cars, through underinsulated homes and glass offices, to energy-intensive machines, factories, and even whole industries, America may be saddled with billions of dollars of increasingly
uneconomical capital investments—all of which were good investments under the assumptions of cheap or free energy.

It is an extreme irony that government policies designed to increase
the well-being of society have left the nation with a capital base that
may become obsolete. The results of such policies in transportation
are clear: cheap energy, a nationally maintained highway system, and
Interstate Commerce Commission regulations have encouraged the
use of trucks over trains, even though trucks are six times more polluting, six times more wasteful of fuel, and add immeasurably to traffic congestion. In another area, the control of the cost of natural gas
led producers to make stoves with pilot lights. Now homes across the
country are stuck with a labor-saving device that consumes fully a
third of the energy used annually by a kitchen range. A final example
is cotton: potentially cheap and plentiful in the United States, cotton
has been largely replaced by nylon and other synthetic fabrics that
require six to ten separate high-energy chemical reactions operating
at temperatures up to 700°.

Energy use in the United States is said to amount to the equivalent
of each American having 300 personal servants. These servants, unfortunately, have begun to engage in featherbedding and other forms
of work restrictions. Between 1900 and 1970, per capita energy use
increased by 400 percent but per capita GNP grew by only 350 percent. Electricity—our fastest growing servant—seems to have lost the
work ethic entirely. Electricity productivity in manufacturing has
declined from 70 cents per kilowatt hour in 1947 to 45 cents in 1967
(in 1958 dollars).[15]

The energy content of goods and services, expressed as the unit of
energy per unit output, may be called *energy intensity.* It is instructive to review some trends in this measure.

Water Supply   The energy cost of providing water to Southern California exemplifies how energy growth occurs for one essential resource. During the first third of this century when irrigation agriculture was expanding rapidly, the energy intensity of water rose from 151 KWH per acre foot in the 1900-1910 period to 211 KWH per acre foot in 1930.[16] In 1973 water from the California aqueduct had an energy intensity of 2600 KWH per acre foot.[17] This represents approximately a 4 percent annual average rate of growth. The reason for this growth is that the people of Southern California have had to reach out farther and farther to obtain the water needed to support the growth of the metropolitan area. First wells and springs sufficed, then the nearby Owens River was tapped, followed by the Colorado, and most recently distant Northern California waters have had to be developed. This growth required energy.

Metals   Increasingly, energy needs have soared to make use of diminishing grades of metal ores. But even more important is the general trend toward using metals with increasingly higher energy content, such as high-grade steels and aluminum. Some of these uses may be regarded as frivolous (aluminum cans); others may result in greater material efficiencies. Whichever is the case, we are using more and more materials with high-energy content (Exhibit 9).[18] Aluminum requires about three times as much energy as copper, and roughly the same energy use ratio applies for the switch from low-grade to high-alloy steels.

Transportation   Transportation represents the largest portion of U.S. energy consumption. It provides essentially a service function for the production of goods. Moreover, the nature of this service is closely associated with time saved, and this has a special significance because transportation energy-intensity tends to grow for any given transport mode as a function of speed. For example, the Concorde SST has about double the energy-intensity of a subsonic jet.[19]

Exhibit 9
Energy Consumption in Basic Materials Processing per Ton of Product

Material	Energy used for production, manufacturing equipment use, and transportation of finished goods (in thermal kilowatt-hours)[a]
Steel	12,600
Aluminum	67,200
Copper	21,000
High-grade steel (silicone and metal) alloys	59,200
Zinc	14,700
Lead	12,900
Electrically processed metals	51,200
Titanium	141,200
Cement	2,300
Sand and gravel	21
Inorganic chemicals	2,700
Finished plate glass	7,200
Plastics	2,900[b]
Paper	6,400
Coal	42
Lumber	1.51 per board foot

Source: English, "The Long-Run Price of Energy Will Be Down"

[a]A thermal kilowatt-hour is an energy measure in electrical terms that takes into account the efficiency of the electrical production and distribution system.
[b]Does not include feedstock.

Food Production   The productivity effects of growing energy-intensity are most thoroughly documented in the agricultural sector of the economy. While America's total energy use has doubled during the past twenty years, it has tripled in some forms of food production. David Pimental has analyzed the effects of this increased energy use on the production of America's largest grain crop, corn.[20] Between 1945 and 1970, corn yields increased a remarkable 240 percent per acre, but energy input increased 310 percent. Pimental estimates that the consequent yield in corn calories per unit of fuel kilocalorie decreased 24 percent in the fifteen years ending in 1970. One result of the heavy use of energy in agriculture is that food in America is the most expensive in the world. If a peasant in India had to purchase his meager diet at U.S. prices, it would cost twice his income.[21]

John and Carol Steinhart have built on Pimental's studies and have traced energy inputs through the entire food system, ranging from its use as fertilizers and pesticides, through such intermediary purposes as processing, packing, and storing, to its delivery at retail stores.[22] They have found that since 1955 increments in food production have been getting smaller despite continuing growth in energy inputs (Exhibit 10).

Moreover, the Steinharts indicate that further substitutions of technology and energy for labor are not likely because use of agricultural labor has bottomed out on an S-curve (Exhibit 11).

Indeed, Pimental and the Steinharts argue that the common assumption about the high productivity of the American farmer ("He feeds 50 people") is a myth. Two nonfarm workers—canners, grocery store clerks, carhops, and so on—are needed to support each farmer. Thus, rather than improving farm productivity by substituting technology for labor as in the classical model, America has in part substituted working at McDonald's for working for farmer McDonald. At best, this is a questionable contribution to the quality of life. Significantly, government subsidies to agriculture (reaching a high of $7.3 billion in 1972) were greatly responsible for the well-publicized rising productivity of the American farmer—and responsible as well for his overuse of energy since 1955. The upshot today is that "agriculture requires 0.011 BTU of human energy in addition to 1.14 BTU of fossil energy to produce only 1.0 BTU of agricultural output."[23]

Pimental and the Steinharts suggest that numerous changes will have to be made in American agricultural practice to increase its energy efficiency. These steps run counter to many of the most basic assumptions of economists. For example, it may be necessary to substitute at least some labor for capital and energy on the farms, and perhaps it may even be necessary to abandon some chemical farming.

Exhibit 10
Farm Output as a Function of Energy Input to the U.S. Food System, 1920 to 1970

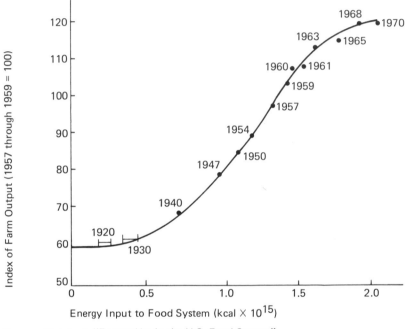

Source: Steinhart, "Energy Use in the U.S. Food System"

Exhibit 11
Substitution of Energy for Labor in U.S. Agriculture

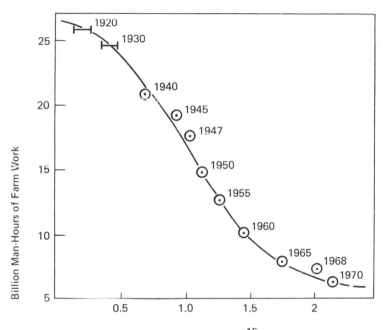

Energy Input to Food System (kcal $\times$ 10^{15})

Source: Steinhart, "Energy Use in the U.S. Food System"

Summary

An overview of the present energy situation in America leads to the conclusion that the nation may now start to pay a high price for the cheap energy available in the past. As Udall, Conconi, and Osterhout argue, the price is being paid not only at the gas pump, but in several less quantifiable and less direct ways as well:

- Domestic oil and gas reserves are being depleted and new sources are not being developed. Because of controls designed to keep energy cheap, U.S. crude oil production has been declining since 1970 and natural gas consumption has been exceeding new discoveries since 1968.

- There is increased reliance on foreign oil supplies. Today, the United States is dependent on foreign oil for about 35 percent of its needs. Energy consumption in the United States is now growing 5 percent more rapidly than growth in domestic supply.

- There is an increase in environmental pollution. Cheap energy led to inefficient practices—such as cars that gave off much of their energy in the form of pollution. Inefficient practices also led to the rapid depletion of cleaner forms of energy (e.g., natural gas). As a result of this depletion, it is now necessary to step up the development of such environmentally questionable resources as surface coal and plutonium.

- Waste and planned obsolescence have been encouraged. America's throwaway economy was based in large part on cheap energy. Approximately three and one half percent of GNP—or $25 billion— is spent on the packaging of goods, 90 percent of which are not recycled. Moreover, it costs about $420 million annually to dispose of this packaging, much of which is not biodegradable.

- Bias for capital/energy-intensive goods has been created. Between 1946 and 1968, population increased by 43 percent and GNP increased by 59 percent. During the same years, the production of electric household items increased 1,040 percent, air conditioner compression units 2,850 percent, synthetic fibers 5,980 percent, and non-

returnable bottles by 53,000 percent. Of course, these increased from
practically zero; the point is that cheap energy facilitated the creation
of entire industries that would not have been developed as rapidly or
at all had energy been dearer.

- Alternative energy technologies have been discouraged. Cheap fossil
  and other capital forms of fuel have discouraged the development of
  alternative technologies to utilize income forms such as solar and
  methane (produced from waste materials).

- In the past, transitions from wood to coal and from whale oil to
  petroleum were relatively smooth because each entailed a switch to a
  cheaper, more abundant, and efficient fuel. Now capital forms are becoming less economical, but there is no income replacement standing
  ready.[24]

What characterizes the U.S. economy and distinguishes it from
other economies is not simply that it uses energy less efficiently but
that it produces goods that are in turn also inefficient energy users.
For example, in the last fifteen years, while Europe and Japan made
important breakthroughs in mass-producing small cars, the United
States continued its historical pattern of producing big cars. From
1960 to 1972, the United States produced ever more autos, more big
autos, and more autos with air conditioning. In addition, Americans
drove these vehicles more miles with each successive year (see Exhibit
12).

Cheap energy has caused American industry to make some major
capital- and energy-intensive transitions over the last thirty years. At
the time, such changeovers (for example, from wood to plastics, from
cotton and wool to synthetic fibers, and from soap to detergents)
seemed not only economically viable but appeared to provide consumers with better products.

After having been lulled into complacency for a generation by government cheap-energy policies, American industry has now been
caught short by the rising price of energy. Having sunk billions into

Exhibit 12
Selected Data on Automobiles, United States, 1960 to 1971

Year	Passenger Cars			
	Registration (X 10^6)	FIAC[a] (%)	Average Use (miles per car)	Fuel (miles per gallon)
1960	61.7	6.9	9,446	14.28
1965	75.2	23.3	9,286	14.15
1968	83.6	43.3	9,448	13.91
1969	86.9	54.0	9,633	13.75
1970	89.2	60.9	9,783	13.58
1971	92.8	61.0	9,926	13.73
1972	96.9	68.6	10,184	13.49

Source: Landsberg, "Low Cost, Abundant Energy"

[a]FIAC: factory-installed air conditioning.

capital-intensive processes on the assumption that these processes would always be fueled by cheap energy, some American industries are seeing their production costs soar dramatically, often indicating a trend that threatens to price their goods out of the market. Indeed, if the government continues its present policy of also trying to force industry to internalize the price of pollution of these same goods, the future portends many severe bouts of economic dislocation. And as if to rub salt in the industrialist's wounds, the American economy is said by many to be caught in a capital crunch that is at once a partial result of the energy situation as well as a cause of it: shortages of capital greatly limit changeovers to less energy-intensive goods and services.

Moreover, industry now finds itself in another bind: not only are many industries on the fringe of becoming uneconomical, but the demand signals sent from society for their products are rapidly changing. Beginning in the late 1960s, increasingly affluent America began to criticize the mass-produced and synthetic goods that had come to symbolize the nation's prosperity. Businessmen, deeply involved with trying to meet the demands of a consumer society for more, were suddenly met with calls to produce less. Almost overnight, the basic values on which economic growth was predicated were being reviled. Such long-accepted measures of well-being as the gross national product, standard of living and industrial efficiency came under increasing challenge. First, members of the counterculture, then upper middle-class intellectuals, and eventually presidents of the United States and presidents of corporations themselves came to talk of a new indicator of gross national weal: the quality of life. Although it is unclear how to measure the quality of life, there is at least some agreement that a quality life cannot be achieved through current practices for exploiting energy and other national resources.

Thus, just as the energy situation started to threaten, it soon became clear that the standard industrial reaction to it—more production of fossil and nuclear fuels—would be seen as trade-offs against environmental and other quality-of-life concerns.

It becomes clear from an examination of America's current energy situation that the resolution of the key issues basically will be a political and social process. The short-term problem is not simply getting enough energy—that can be accomplished readily enough. Rather, the problem is providing energy in a way that is compatible with the social values and economic aspirations of the nation. This is a challenge not likely to be met in the near future because the values, goals, and economic priorities of powerful groups in America are competing and conflicting—and there is no sign of willingness to coalesce around a common agenda. Consequently, any successful energy policy will have to measure up well against the following often conflicting performance criteria:

- Conservation of energy and natural resources

- Reduction of pollution

- Decrease of unemployment

- Maintenance of a high standard of living

- Retention of tolerable rates of inflation

- Preservation of individual liberty and a free market economy

In the short run, at least, no energy policy seems entirely capable of satisfying these criteria. It is against this unhopeful political backdrop that the future of energy policy will be played out.

3. The Near Future: Mitigated Pessimism

In any field of scientific endeavor, anything that can possibly go wrong will go wrong.

Left to themselves, things always go from bad to worse.

If there is a possibility of several things going wrong, the one that will go wrong is the one that will do the most damage.

Murphy's Laws

If you talk about the future, even the demons will laugh.

Traditional Japanese Saying

When historians write about the past and journalists report present-day happenings, they draw on a body of data or facts. Though there is always some room for disagreement over what constitutes fact, the most important human disagreements are over interpretations of those facts. These value judgments eventually determine public policy and private practices. Presumably, if one has his facts straight, he will make better choices than if he applied his system of values to misinformation. There is no objective or scientific way of proving the rightness or wrongness of the value system of a Chairman Mao of China or a Chairman Geneen of ITT, but we can objectively measure whether each chairman has the best information available before he makes an important decision.

Analysis of the future is an especially value-laden pursuit. Because so few objective data about the future are available, there is seldom a factual basis for making decisions. For this reason, long-range planners seek to build data bases about the future, realizing that an imperfect base is better than no base at all. In the first two chapters of this report, the data base was published information about the past and present (the choice of what data to use and how to interpret them was, of course, based on our values). In the following chapters about the future we literally have had to create a data base.

A Note about the Delphi Technique
One way to create a data base about the future is to identify those individuals with the best objective expertise about the past and present and to poll their opinions about how they see the future of their

disciplines developing. The opinion survey method used in this study was the Delphi technique, a method for obtaining a consensus from a panel of experts that avoids the jury-room effect typical of face-to-face discussion. In a Delphi study, a panel of experts is presented with a questionnaire that asks them to respond individually (and preferably in numerical terms) to a series of questions. The responses to this initial questionnaire are collated and the results are fed back to the panelists. The panelists are then asked to review their previous estimates in the light of the distribution of responses of their colleagues. They are also asked to state their reasons for their estimates, particularly if these are near one or the other end of the distribution of panel responses. This process is repeated for several rounds until, typically, the spread of opinion among panelists is substantially reduced. The median of the last round of estimates is accepted as the consensus of the panelists if the responses are not still widely disparate.

The anonymous debate generated in the Delphi technique reduces the influence of such psychological factors as specious persuasion, the unwillingness to abandon publicly expressed judgments, and the bandwagon effects of majority opinion.

The Delphi survey used in this study generated over 320 separate forecasts from three expert panels on technology, economics, and society. The fifty-four experts from academia, business, and government who constituted the panels reached a reasonable consensus on all but about forty of the items presented to them during three iterations of the process. Of course, the consensus of their opinions does not constitute "facts" about the future—it merely represents the best guesses of the most qualified people we could identify and persuade to take part in the Delphi. (The findings of the Delphi panel are reported in Chapter 5.)

In general, what is remarkable about our Delphi forecasts is that they tend to be rather more optimistic than the gloom-and-doom energy prognostications for the economy and society that have made headlines over the last three years. Even such a normally sanguine figure as Edward Teller (who has seemed to many to be the Pangloss of the nuclear age) is given to foreboding language:

Within the United States, we are threatened by acute shortages which may be caused by a new oil embargo or by an interruption of sea traffic. The energy shortage will cause a further slowdown of our economy and could lead to its collapse. Cold homes, a gasoline shortage, increase of unemployment and troubles with foreign exchange are some of the possible consequences. An epidemic of bankruptcies similar to those that occurred in the 1930s cannot be excluded.

Month by month the outlook has become darker. The winter embargo of 1973-1974 found us in a relatively strong position. A new shortage may do much more damage. Increasing inflation may wipe out all savings. Unemployment may easily exceed the 10 million figure. The post-war generation—which has never experienced real hardship—may find out what deprivation and hunger mean.

Domestic disturbances may become severe, but the situation abroad is worse. Payment of $100 billion per year to the Organization of Petroleum Exporting Countries (OPEC) members and formation of surplus capital in the Arab OPEC countries ($60 billion in 1974) is a danger signal. Italy and England are on the verge of insolvency. The almost complete dependence of Japan on imported energy will cause profound damage. The tripling of fertilizer prices may bring about the starvation of millions more on the subcontinent of India and elsewhere. Trouble and despair abroad are bound to react on our own country.[1]

On the other end of the political spectrum, Dall Forsythe writes in the radical journal *Working Papers* that

Along with . . . transformations in industrial machinery and power generating capacity will come changes in social patterns. As industries die or move closer to new power sources (near coal fields, for example), workers will lose jobs or, if their skills are valuable enough, they will uproot their families and follow their factories. As transportation costs rise, we will increasingly rely on locally produced goods and food, and our economy will begin to become less and less national and more and more regional. Commuting will become too costly for any but the wealthy to afford. Suburbanites may move back to the cities; or industries, especially white-collar ones, may accelerate their moves to the suburbs. In the face of continuing social and economic uncertainty, stock markets will remain volatile and depressed.

In all, I believe we will face an extended period of what can only be characterized as social and economic chaos. One student of revolutions argues that such conditions are often the proximate cause of large-scale political upheavals. . . .

These social and economic changes will undoubtedly produce changes in political consciousness. We are likely to see the rebirth of the kind of class-based political alignments that characterized earlier periods of scarcity in America.[2]

Although the positions of the advocates of more (those who stress the value of economic growth) and the advocates of less (those who stress quality-of-life concerns) are often at seemingly irreconcilable odds, the two sides were fused in a common bond of near panic by the implementation of the Arab oil embargo and the subsequent rise in petroleum prices. The so-called oil crisis at least made one thing clear: no group wishes to pay higher prices or to make painful trade-offs to achieve the priority items on their social and economic agendas.

As a nation, nothing brought us together in a more emphatic way than the end of the era of cheap energy. The future looks bleak in almost everyone's view. On one side, higher energy prices are viewed as worrying because they portend

- A decline in GNP and real standard of living

- Greater government control over the decisions of individuals and enterprises

- An increasing capital shortage

- Economic dislocations

- Increased dependence on the OPEC and other international resource cartels

- An increase in inflation

- On the other side, higher energy prices are generating fear of

- Increased environmental pollution

- A worsening of unemployment and poverty

- Potential of nuclear accidents

- An oil war

- Depletion of natural resources

- Exacerbation of the world food problem

On all sides, there is now wide-based acceptance that Murphy's Laws reign supreme: whatever can go wrong, will go wrong. Our Delphi study, however, indicates that such pessimism may be over-stated. In the short run, it seems that the effects of rising energy prices on GNP, unemployment, poverty, inflation, economic disloca-tions, and capital availability will probably not be as great as was feared at the height of the oil embargo. The price for higher energy bills will have to be paid, of course, and this often will entail some belt tightening, sacrifice, and painful trade-offs—but the price can be paid without undercutting the social and economic strength of the nation.

Economic Effects of Rising Energy Prices
The most hotly debated issue of the energy situation is the likely effect of rising energy prices on the economy. Such concern is under-standable. Economic changes often send out severe social and politi-

cal ripples. Economic changes are felt in the pocketbooks of all Americans. And, perhaps most singularly, economic changes can be quantified; hence, economic measures are a widely accepted thermometer of the health of the nation.

Today it is the common economic wisdom that increased energy use is necessary for economic growth. The Council of Economic Advisers, for example, estimates that a reduction in oil imports by 1 million barrels per day would lower GNP by $15 billion and would cost 400,000 jobs.[3] But is the correlation between increased energy use and the economic health of the nation this strong and clear? The two factors may not be quite as closely linked as the nation's economic leadership has assumed.

Effects on GNP   A controversial econometric model designed by Data Resources, Inc. (DRI), has projected that cutting energy growth in half from the recent twenty-year historical rate of 3.4 percent annually would have only a minimally negative effect on GNP, and would raise the inflation rate only 0.2 percent annually. The DRI econometricians achieve the energy savings in their model not through rationing but through higher energy prices. They argue that reduced energy use in the future will have only a slight effect on GNP because energy use increased in the past not because it was needed but because it was cheap. (In the twenty-year period ending in 1971, real electricity prices fell 43 percent, refined petroleum prices 17 percent, and coal prices 15 percent.) Toward the end of this period the growth rate of energy use had increased from a little over 3 percent to over 4 percent, but the amount of energy needed to produce one dollar of GNP did not increase after 1955. The DRI model assumes that industrial energy use is price-elastic, and the increases in prices will lead to economical, energy-saving substitutions of capital for energy (such as insulation), replenishable materials for energy (wood for plastics) and labor for energy (handmade goods for assembly-made goods), without a real effect on productivity or life-styles.

The USC Delphi panel is not quite as sanguine as the DRI econometricians. Most basically, the panel feels that the demand for electricity is not as price-elastic as the DRI study assumes. The Delphi panel assumes that a doubling of the price of energy would lead to about a 20 percent reduction in demand, while the DRI study assumes reduction of around 40 percent. The Delphi study is also less optimistic about the correlation between the growth rates of energy consumption and the growth of GNP. The Delphi consensus is that a 2.67 percent annual growth rate in energy use would correlate with the 3 percent growth rate in GNP they predict for the next decade. Along with this, the panel forecasts an average inflation rate of 5 percent annually for the next decade. Thus, the Delphic view of America's economic future through 1985—inflation rate 5 percent; real GNP growth 3 percent; energy growth 2.67 percent—may not be as rosy as the DRI econometric forecast, but it does not portend catastrophe.[5] The Delphi panel says that if a severe worldwide depression does not occur by the year 1977 (and they offer only a 10 percent probability for this event) a 1930s-type depression will *not* occur in the foreseeable future. They also see very little likelihood of the U.S. petroleum industry being nationalized. They forecast that the annual rate of U.S. population growth will fall to 0.6 percent by 1985. They feel that relative energy prices will rise faster than prices for industrial raw materials, which in turn will rise faster than prices for food. The relative cost of labor will drop considerably against these three measures. As a result, they see employment increasing as some labor is substituted for capital and energy.

Not a great ten years to anticipate, but in the perspective of world history perhaps a rather good decade. Indeed, it may only appear bad because we are comparing the present and near future to a recent past that was in many ways a historical aberration. During no time in recent history was energy as cheap and abundant as it was during the last two decades. Historically in the United States, per capita energy use had grown one-third more slowly than per capita GNP. Only in the last twenty years did energy use grow at the same rate as GNP. This means the United States had energy to burn in the last twenty years, which gave the impression of a superabundant economy. Actually, the efficiency of energy use was dropping during these periods, but this fact was masked by energy's artificially low price, which in turn was a kind of subsidy to a heated-up consumer economy. The Delphi forecast indicates that it is *not* now necessary to go back to a preconsumer economy, but that the phenomenal, superheated, and wasteful growth of the last two decades will probably not be the pattern of the future.

A 3 percent rate of growth is not as attractive as 4 percent or 5 percent, of course, but the slower rate may not have all the negative effects in the future that we have come to associate with slow growth in the past.[6] In a recent study Mazur and Rosa argue that energy consumption, GNP, and the quality of life are not as closely intertwined as we have feared.[7]

They argue that although there is a strong correlation between a country's GNP and its energy consumption, the correlation is not causation. This can be demonstrated by comparing the correlation between per capita energy consumption, GNP, and quality-of-life measures between developed countries and underdeveloped countries versus the same comparisons among developed countries only. As expected, in Japan, West Germany, and the United States, the quality of life, GNP, and energy consumption are all higher than in Iraq, Uganda, or Nepal. But comparisons among developed countries only show a very weak correlation among these measures. For example, Luxembourg and the United States use much more energy per capita than do Japan and Sweden, but the quality of life in all four countries does not differ greatly. Japan uses about four times less energy than the United States, but its rate of economic growth has been about three times that of the United States.

How can these anomalies be explained? Mazur and Rosa suggest that in some cases increased GNP may cause increases in energy consumption rather than vice versa. Alternatively, both GNP and energy consumption may simply be measures of industrialization without a causal nexus. One conclusion seems to be emerging from many recent

studies: once a nation is industrialized, it may be able to cut back on
energy consumption. In the short run, this will lead to a slight negative effect on GNP; in the long run it could improve the quality of
life.

Businessmen and politicians, of course, live in the short run.

Effects on Specific Industries   It is evident that many short-term economic dislocations will result from higher energy prices. It is commonly assumed that many energy-intensive industries are likely to be
adversely affected, including airlines, autos, recreation vehicles, steel,
cement, aluminum, plastics, cleaning products, and utilities. But
other industries—better positioned with regard to energy utilization—
will benefit, including coal, railways, water transportation, auto
parts, bicycles, oil-drilling equipment, energy engineering, communications, computers, batteries, building insulation, furnaces, furniture,
apparels, and shoes and other leather products.

Such assumptions are dangerous without careful analysis. The more
specific one is about forecasting the future, the more likely one is to
be wrong. Some generalizations, however, have rather high probabilities. For example, the greatest impact of reduced energy availability
is likely to be felt in large concentrated industries. These industries
are typically very capital-intensive, a posture that was in part encouraged by the availability of abundant and cheap energy. Their capital
plant and equipment are highly specialized and represent a largely
irreversible investment decision in the short run. The costs of adjustment to a less energy-intensive mode are extremely high, especially if
adjustment is attempted over a short time. Their demand for energy,
then, tends to be very inelastic. Thus, victimized by costs beyond
their control and unable to adjust, many of these industries face production price increases, production cutbacks, and reduced profits.[8]

Under this scenario, an interesting phenomenon could occur: a reversal of the seemingly immutable trend of increasing economic dominance by concentrated industries. Growth—the single most important industrial goal of the corporate giants—would cease or slow down

relative to that in the less capital-intensive industries that are characterized by smaller firms and more competition. In a word, there
could be less concentration in the American economy.

This possible trend in the economy will be heightened, according
to the Delphi panel, by the more vigorous antitrust actions that will
accompany prolonged energy scarcity. The panel also forecasts the
following government actions:

- Possible nationalization of some business sectors

- Increase in the regulation of exchange of goods

- Increase in consumer protection and pollution controls

- Increased regulation of multinational corporations

The panel feels that the trend in America has for some time been in
the direction of more government activity in the marketplace and
that energy scarcity will heighten this activity. According to Gallup
and other polls, Americans have not trusted big business for some
time, and the energy crisis apparently confirmed and exacerbated
these feelings.

As Irving Kristol and other friends of American business have been
warning, the most profound second-order consequence of the energy
crisis may come about as the result of changed perceptions and attitudes of the citizenry.[9] The Congress, Kristol warns, will take its signals from the public concerning increased regulation and even nationalization of business. If the public continues to feel (as it has in the
last few years) that oil corporations manipulated the energy crisis and
profiteered at its expense, then such attitudes would strengthen the
hand of those in the Congress who oppose big business on ideological
grounds. Kristol's message is not an attack on big business. Rather,
he says that the future of government activity in the marketplace is
very much in the hands of businessmen themselves. To the extent
that businessmen impress Americans that they are acting in the public interest, the Congress will follow the will of the public and not increase the current heavy regulatory load.

The most immediate threat to the status quo appears to be a series
of proposed changes in the Congress to promote greater competition
in the energy industries. It is increasingly argued that both horizontal
and vertical integration in the energy industries tends to reduce competition. To the American public, it often seems that oil, gas, coal,
and uranium companies should be separate institutions. A single company seems to have little incentive to pursue new products that compete with its major profit lines. It is also argued that similar disincentives may exist in vertically integrated companies that seek deposits,
extract and refine the product, and then wholesale and distribute it
to their own retail stores. Two other structural changes—national
energy companies to compete in the major energy fields, and a national oil company to conduct all international energy transactions—
are also gaining support in Congress. The economic facts that might
justify such horizontal and vertical integration are increasingly irrele-
vant in a charged atmosphere in which the demand to create any energy policy has taken precedence over the demand for an effective
energy policy.

Most likely, the perceived attitudes of the public rather than objective analysis will tip the Congress one way or the other on these
issues. And, if Kristol is correct, the posture of the energy companies
may anger the American public into support of congressional efforts
to increase competition.

On the other hand, the dislocations likely to occur as the result of
higher energy prices could have an astringent effect on the American
capitalistic system, flushing out inefficient industries and forcing the
nation to concentrate on its strengths. For some time it has been
clear that America's competitive advantages in the world lie in agriculture, services, high technology, and knowledge industries.

With the exception of agriculture, all these industries are relatively
energy-efficient, nonpolluting, and labor-intensive. (And, as we have
seen, agriculture might be improved on all three measures without
sacrificing productivity.) Higher priced energy will strengthen these
industries while at the same time weakening industries that rely on
the outdated middle-range technologies that characterize mass pro-

duction. (See Chapter 4 for more detail on technological choice.) Not only do many of these anachronistic technologies waste energy and pollute, they are capital-intensive and tend to offer a mix of jobs that offer little satisfaction to workers. (Some Delphi panelists even asked why America should be in some mass-production industries when other nations can supply us with the needed goods at a lower price.)

Change is a strength of the capitalist system. Higher energy prices will force change. The challenge to American businessmen is to manage the change in a creative way that minimizes the negative dislocative effects that by necessity must occur. Significantly, the Delphi panel seems confident that American business is capable of accomplishing this change in a resourceful and economic fashion.

Effects on Inflation—Two Views   An increase in the price of energy, ceteris paribus, will be inflationary. Consequently, any policy that seeks to redress the current energy situation through letting prices rise will be considered inflationary and thus probably rejected as politically unfeasible. But will higher energy prices necessarily be inflationary? To the extent that the Delphi panel does not see the rate of inflation dipping below 5 percent for the next decade, the answer is yes. The question is whether the rate can be held to this high but still acceptable level.

There is some reason for optimism here. First, ceteris paribus is an incorrect assumption. Higher energy prices will cause individuals and industries to conserve, substitute, and do without. Through these changing industrial practices and individual behaviors, the efficiency of the system may actually increase. Experiences at Dow Chemical and elsewhere indicate that the costs of energy in some industrial processes can drop as the result of better housekeeping activities— even when prices rise. How much efficiency can be improved by such practices is limited, however. The Delphi panel feels that the average efficiency of energy utilization will only increase by about 5 percent every ten years.

The largest inflationary threat to the economy as the result of higher energy prices is the likely substitution of some labor for capital and energy. (See Chapter 4 for a further explanation of this phenomenon.) If past experience is a guide, inflation has been checked in Western economies through increases in productivity that resulted from substitutions of capital and energy for labor. By reversing the process, will the American economy further exacerbate its current low-productivity/high-inflation situation? It is not clear that the obvious answer—yes—will be the correct answer for the future.

The relationship of labor to productivity and inflation is as murky as it is controversial. Consequently, whether one speaks from the perspective of organized labor, management, or a neutral position, it is easy to misstate the contribution of workers to these factors. Perhaps the most damaging industrial myth is that productivity of nations and of enterprises hinges on how hard employees work.[10] Often this myth is fueled by executives who wish to cover up the results of their mismanagement by passing the buck, by trade unionists who wish to share in productivity gains to which workers made no contribution, and by behavioral scientists who wish to sell job enrichment and other motivational nostrums as ways to increase productivity. In fact, the productivity of firms is largely determined by technology and the strategic planning, marketing, finance, and research decisions of management.

Specifically with regard to inflation, some argue that the worker in his role as a consumer is of paramount importance. That is, a raise in a worker's wage will usually have less effect on the price of the goods he produces than his increased purchasing power will have on feeding inflation indirectly. Thus, the argument goes, substitutions of labor for capital may not be as inflationary as some fear—particularly because most such substitutions would occur in job categories where wages are lowest.[11]

It is also frequently asserted that inflation is more often caused by the overextension of bank credit to stimulate capital investment than it is by the failure of inefficient labor-intensive industries to automate their physical plants. Indeed, some marginal substitutions of labor for capital might even have a somewhat mitigating effect on inflation if the substitutions dampen the demand for the creation of new money.

Many businessmen and economists feel that high inflation and low productivity in the United States have come about because American managers do not invest as much capital per worker as do their Japanese and German counterparts. International comparisons are always risky, but it may well be that the United States has reached the point in its economic development where increased capital investments do not have the high payoff they have in foreign lands. What may account for the international differences in investment per worker is that the bulk of new jobs being created in the United States are in the labor-intensive services sector, while Japan and Europe (not yet post-industrial economies) are still creating the bulk of their jobs in heavy industry where the cost of creating jobs is higher.

Moreover, as has been argued above, the United States may also be reaching the point of diminishing returns in its search for greater productivity through the use of more energy in industry. For example, productivity increases have not kept pace with the use of electricity in manufacturing. Kilowatt use per man has increased sixteen times in the last half century, while productivity has increased only seven times.[12] Thus the relationship between energy use and productivity may be as tenuous as the relationship between labor-intensity and productivity. As stated above, the United States uses more energy per capita than Japan whose rates of both productivity and employment are much higher than ours. This proves nothing, of course, except that the relationships between the factors of production are not economic laws; more accurately, they may be thought of as paradoxes.

Clearly, there are many unknowns in the relationship among energy, inflation, and productivity, but the Delphi panel feels that the relative cost of energy will rise faster than the cost of labor. What this means, ceteris paribus, is that without some kind of change in the mix of factors of production (such as substituting labor or energy-saving capital or materials for energy) the rising costs of energy will most likely drive up the price of goods and thus fuel inflation. However, the Delphi panel feels that businessmen will make such changes and thus dampen the inflationary aspects of higher energy prices.

There is another side to this coin, however. Selwyn Enzer argues that the presence of OPEC and of such structural factors as indexing in the American economy will prevent the marketplace from achieving greater efficiency in the use of energy resources, promoting conservation, stimulating the search for new deposits, and developing new energy sources.[13] Though classic economic thinking would predict such effects, on closer inspection it appears to Enzer quite likely that the market cannot work to reduce the inflationary aspects of high-price petroleum, because the United States presently has very little control over the price of energy in general and petroleum in particular. Although we can theoretically control the price of domestic production, this control is being eroded by the presence of the OPEC cartel. As opposed to a price established in a competitive market with many buyers and many sellers, the OPEC monopoly determines prices on the basis of the elasticity of demand and the cost and availability of substitutes. The near-term impact of the abrupt increases in OPEC oil has been to stimulate inflation, which in turn resulted in price escalations in virtually all the world commodities, including domestic oil and gas. Consequently, much of the debate over decontrolling domestic prices may be a current version of jawboning.

Other new economic forces are also being brought into play. These include increased prices in exports generally. The price of food on the international markets, for example, has perhaps tripled since oil prices rose. This chain reaction of price increases is viewed by some as a means by which the oil consumers hope to inflate away the economic impact of their energy burden. In any event, the realities of the economic interdependence of the nations of the world make it highly unlikely for a nation, even one as large as the United States, to insulate its domestic economy from price rises in as basic a commodity as oil.

The important issue is whether increases in the price of energy will promote the efficiencies, conservation, and search for new options that longer-term needs demand. Classic economic theory describing the dynamics of the free marketplace suggests that an increase in energy prices will promote these developments, but we may no longer have the kind of marketplace on which classic economic theory is based. Two very important constraints on the functioning of the market have developed over the last decade.

First, virtually automatic price adjustment mechanisms largely offset the higher cost of energy. Energy-consuming industries, even the regulated industries, have been generally granted pass-through price-increase privileges for higher energy costs. Given such privileges, what effect do higher energy costs have in promoting economies? If airlines, for example, can pass their increased petroleum costs on to customers, they are less motivated to phase out lightly traveled routes or to press for route-swapping privileges that can lead to greater efficiency through higher load factors. As long as all the competitors have recourse to the same remedies, the incentives for change sought from higher prices in the factors of production are likely to be minimal.

In the product and services market we find another form of indexing. These hide under the rubric of cost-of-living adjustments. Congress, for example, which has virtually institutionalized cost-of-living adjustments in social security and other benefits programs, has recently institutionalized it even for their own incomes. Clearly the need to reduce consumption of an essential commodity whose cost has increased is greatly reduced in the presence of offsetting increases in income.

The second difference likely to occur in the real marketplace is that such energy-saving substitutions as labor for energy-consuming devices and communications for travel may not occur to the degree that theory would suggest. Energy price increases and the automatic adjustment mechanisms are so pervasive that all prices are affected almost in unison. Thus the price of substitutes may rise almost as fast as energy-intensive prices rise.

It is not clear that Enzer's pessimistic view of inflation is a more accurate view of reality than the more optimistic Delphic view, but there can be no doubt that the existence of OPEC and indexing are considerable stumbling blocks to the reduction of inflation.

Effects on Capital Availability   During the next ten or more years, the United States is faced with the problem of supplying an adequate and dependable quantity of traditional fuels to keep the economy running. Conservation alone will not obviate the need to drill new oil and gas wells, build new plants for coal gasification, shale oil conversion, and geothermal and nuclear power.

The technology exists for developing and operating these types of energy-producing facilities. The immediate challenge facing the energy industries is not so much technological as it is finding the investment dollars required to carry out the exploration and development, building of facilities, and opening of mines that will lead to additional sources of energy. In the United States, there now exist the makings of an energy conundrum:

- Without economic growth, there is no new capital formation.

- Without capital formation, there are no new energy resources.

- Without new energy resources, there is no economic growth.

The current projections of the capital requirements needed to achieve an adequate supply of energy without overreliance on OPEC oil vary with the technical assumptions on which they are based. But most projections reach the same conclusion: the size and scope of the new or continued investment in energy over the next ten years will be staggering.

The Federal Energy Administration's estimates on financing Project Independence illustrate the magnitude of the necessary investment requirements. Specifically, the report indicates that energy self-sufficiency can be achieved through the investment of approximately $550 to $630 billion in energy-related industries during the 1974-

1985 period. These figures are perhaps low compared with other projections for capital requirements for this period, projections that presumably have as a goal something less than self-sufficiency (see Exhibit 13).

Capital expenditures by domestic energy industries exceeding $600 billion between 1975 and 1985 are difficult to visualize. Putting the size of these financial requirements into perspective, Project Apollo put U.S. spacemen on the moon for a bargain price of $25 billion.

The Federal Reserve Board has forecasted America's economic future for the next decade. Projections using their model indicate that the economy will be able to support these increased energy capital requirements. The model assumes abrupt increases in oil prices but forecasts that the economy will react in retaliatory ways to the higher costs of energy.[14]

The Federal Reserve Board model also assumes that surpluses in future federal budgets will enable the business community to compete for funds in the capital market. Additionally, shrinking supplies of federal securities will cause a shift by investors toward bank deposits.

It is growing increasingly clear from such studies that because of rising energy prices (and accompanying financial insecurity) capital markets will revert to the relative safety of institutional intermediaries. When times are normal the risks of direct investment seem relatively small. But in periods of rapid change investors look to sources of stability for some kinds of guarantees. Chief among these sources of security are the commercial banks—which thus become the private

Exhibit 13
Estimates of Capital Requirements for Energy Industries, 1975 to 1985

Ford Foundation Report	$1.7 trillion ($1.4 trillion with conservation)
Committee for Economic Development	$600 to $700 billion
Chase Manhattan Bank	$1.2 trillion
Committee on Critical Choices	$800 billion
Federal Energy Administration	$550 to $630 billion

institutions most likely to benefit from the short-term energy squeeze.

Banks have long been the primary instrument of government financial policy. This means that the greater the role of banks in the capital markets, the greater control government has over these markets. With the economic dislocations created by scarce energy, it is likely that government will start to exercise as much control over capital markets as possible. Toward this end, government could provide banks with an increased ability to acquire deposits and issue debts, allow loan expansion, and perhaps loosen some restrictive regulations that currently confine bank activities. The result could be to increase greatly the power of the banks in the economy, which could lead to increased financial concentration and to greater bank holdings in industrial firms.

In short, it seems that private debt financing is likely to continue in the future with more power accruing to the banks—and indirectly to the government.

The federal debt as a percentage of GNP has been declining consistently as a portion of total debt since World War II. By 1985, the Federal Reserve Board expects this debt to decline to 10.5 percent of GNP. Offsetting this decline in federal debt is a projected growth in business debt. In the future, rising corporate debt is anticipated to continue as a major means of financing capital projects (see Exhibit 14).

Exhibit 14
Structure of Outstanding Debt as Percentage of GNP

	1959	1973	1985
Total debt	144.6	144.2	142.9
U.S. government	48.5	26.5	10.5
State and local	13.6	14.1	14.9
Residential	30.1	35.1	37.0
Household—Nonresidential	14.8	19.1	20.3
Business—Nonresidential	33.2	44.1	54.7

Source: Taylor, "A Financial Background for Project Independence"

To finance capital expenditures and working capital requirements adequately and at the same time maintain debt at existing 1973 levels would require new equity financing on the order of $18 billion in 1974 and up to $35 billion in 1980. This can be compared to the paltry $6 billion of equity issues in 1974. Although net equity offerings were considerably stronger in both 1971 and 1972, only $10 billion was raised in each of those years.

Historical rates of equity financing clearly are inadequate to meet the projected needs for energy investment. Inasmuch as the Federal Reserve Board model envisages no such volume of equity financing occurring before 1985, business financing is anticipated to be structured much as it has been over the past several years—resulting inevitably in a further growth of corporate debt from 44 percent of GNP in 1973 to 55 percent of GNP in 1985.

Still, the Federal Energy Administration, the Brookings Institution, the Federal Reserve Board, and others conclude that the needed investment capital will be available for the expansionary requirements of the energy industries through 1985 (Exhibit 15). However, Brookings, the Federal Energy Administration, and the Federal Reserve Board readily admit that projected federal budget surpluses represent the critical factor of stability enabling businesses to finance their en-

Exhibit 15
Estimate of Capital Availability for Energy Investment—Federal Reserve Board Model
(Billions of dollars)

Year	1973	1974	1975	1976
GNP	1,294			
Estimated GNP[a]		1,346	1,399	1,455
Estimated Funds Available for Energy Investment[b]	32	34	35	36
Accumulated Funds Available for Energy Investment	32	66	101	137

Source: *FEA Draft Report on Capital Needs and Federal Policy*

[a]The increase in GNP is computed at an annual increasing rate of 4 percent in constant 1973 dollars.

[b]Estimated fixed business investment in energy-related activities is computed at 2.5 percent of GNP. This represents the 23 percent historical rate of investment in energy-related investments within the fixed business investment component of GNP.

ergy projects.[15] Because such surpluses are often projected but seldom materialize, this assumption leaves the optimism about meeting
capital needs open to some criticism.

Spurred by recent record profits arising from the increased price of
petroleum products, the oil industry has responded to the energy situation by intensifying its efforts to discover and develop new and
alternative sources of energy (Exhibit 16). To meet the country's energy demands, the U.S. petroleum industry budgeted a record $19.5
billion for capital investment in 1974 alone.

The capital budgets of the industry represent a 30 percent increase
over the spending levels of $15 billion in 1973. The increase takes on
added meaning when compared with spending levels of $12.7 billion
for 1972 (see Exhibit 17).

The major emphasis of spending in 1974 centered on oil exploration and production. Sixty percent of total expenditures were allocated to these two activities alone. The allotment for drilling and exploration amounted to $7.66 billion, which is greater than the total
capital spending for all oil industry activity in 1971. These funds
were allocated to financing the drilling of over 30,000 new oil and gas
wells during 1974.

Despite the large increases in income earned during the first half

1977	1978	1979	1980	1981	1982	1983	1984	1985
1,514	1,574	1,637	1,703	1,770	1,841	1,915	1,992	2,072
38	39	41	43	44	46	48	50	52
175	214	255	298	342	388	436	486	538

Exhibit 16
How Oil Profits and Outlays Are Climbing[a]

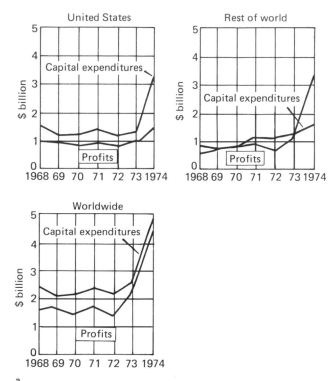

^aFirst quarter 1974 results for 30 U.S. companies.

Source: Chase Manhattan Bank

Exhibit 17
U.S. Oil Company Capital Spending
(Millions of dollars)

	1974 (Budgeted)	Percentage change (1974 vs 1973)	1973 (Estimated)	1972
Exploration and production				
Drilling and exploration	7,668.9	+ 16.3	6,591.0	5,717.6
Production	1,264.9	+ 16.4	1,086.4	942.4
OCS lease bonus	3,200.0	+ 3.8	3,082.0	2,268.8
Total	12,133.8	+ 12.8	10,759.4	8,918.8
Others				
Refining	2,121.0	+ 88.8	1,123.3	946.6
Petrochemicals	599.6	+ 80.9	331.4	300.6
Marketing	839.3	− 7.9	969.9	1,148.9
Natural gas pipelines	650.0	+ 8.3	600.0	578.0
Crude-products pipelines	1,100.0	+633.3	150.0	94.0
Other transportation	345.2	+ 28.8	267.9	175.0
Miscellaneous	1,688.1	+ 89.6	890.4	570.0
Grand Total	19,531.0	+ 29.4	15,092.3	12,731.9

Source: *Oil and Gas Journal*, "Record Capital Oil Outlays Aimed at Easing Shortages"

of 1974, industry profits are not expected to keep pace with future capital expansion plans. By all accounts, 1974 was an aberration in the financial history of the oil companies (Exhibit 18).

In the future, inflationary trends indicate that current charges for depreciation will not cover the replacement of plants and facilities built in earlier years. To duplicate a refinery that cost $100 million twenty years ago might cost $200 to $300 million today. And although inflation is a problem that affects all industry, it is particularly troublesome for capital-intensive industries like the energy industry, which is characterized by costly long-lived facilities.

Moreover, the need to replace low-cost petroleum reserves by new energy sources contributes to the added costs of exploration and production. The lowest cost gas and oil have already been developed and

Exhibit 18
First Half 1974 Profits and Capital Spending
(Millions of dollars)

	Profits	Capital Spending
Exxon	1,555	1,618
Texaco	1,049	1,060
Mobil	626	826
Gulf	540	732
Indiana Standard	499	1,000
Shell	246	464
Arco	233	500
Philips	232	328
Sun	218	375
Conoco	209	335
Getty	135	183
Marathon	80	117

Source: *Oil and Gas Journal*, "Companies' Spending Tops First Half Profits"

replacements for these resources will be far costlier to exploit. Environmental constraints also threaten to reduce energy industry earnings. Consequently, the energy industries have significant doubts that they will be able to generate the funds necessary to finance their tremendous capital expansion programs.

Our conclusions about capital availability tend to be more optimistic than those of the government and the energy industries. First, the Delphi panel believes that the annual requirement of the U.S. energy industry will be more on the order of $60 billion in 1985, rather than the $70 to $100 billion forecast in other studies. Apparently, the panel foresees greater future use of less capital-intensive technologies—such as advanced batteries and methanol—while others see the industry pursuing such costly sources as coal liquefaction, shale, tar sands, and, in the long run, nuclear fusion. Second, we do not assume that the current capital crunch is a permanent fixture of the American economy. The USC study by Wayne Clark finds room for optimism, even under the following untoward assumptions that, (1) the historic growth rates in energy consumption will continue; (2) 40 percent of all industrial capital needs must be financed externally; (3) there will be a 3.6 percent growth in the need for external capital; and (4) OPEC will still be drawing masses of capital out of the U.S. economy. Even under these assumptions, Clark finds private energy firms in the United States capable of meeting their capital requirements.[16]

Another source of potential easing of the capital crunch is the possible shift away from the dominance of the giant heavy industries in the American economy. This class of industry produces 15 percent of the GNP, but uses a third of the total energy in the United States and accounts for over 50 percent of new industrial capital requirements.[17] With some of these companies starting to grow at a slower rate and with presumably a large pool of retained earnings, their demand for funds from the capital markets would drop dramatically. Even with lower interest rates, these firms probably would not be able to absorb the available funds. These funds would then seek new outlets, which would include smaller firms and the most competitive energy industries. The preferred loan status of the large firms would thus be lost, and the capital markets would return to a greater degree of homogeneity. The increasingly dormant regional markets might even be revitalized, and institutional intermediaries would return to their former dominant position, bringing increased market stability. The general level of interest rates probably would be lower.

Although almost all economic indicators seem to support the notion of a capital shortage, there remain certain logical inconsistencies with the notion. What is meant by the word *shortage* in an economic sense? Ultimately, no doubt, there is a real shortage of oil—that is, the amount in the ground is finite. Because the total world reserve of oil is fixed, it is thus meaningful to speak of shortages and to advocate increasing the supply of alternative sources of energy as a policy response to the shortage. But only things in nature are in finite supply; ideas, concepts, and other human products are theoretically limitless. That is why talk about shortages of such things as jobs, social inventions, and even capital has a certain naive ring to it—all these things can be created.

This suggests the need for an alternative way of framing the problem. For example, it often turns out that apparently simple cases of shortages can be better understood and acted on if they are seen as complex problems of maldistribution. Recent attempts to increase the supply of medical manpower illustrate this phenomenon. In the late 1960s, American medical schools made a concerted effort to gain a windfall increase in federal aid by convincing the American public that there was an acute shortage of doctors. This alarmist tactic almost worked—until more thoughtful analysis showed that the problem is more a maldistribution of doctors by both specialty and geography than a general shortage across the board. That is, Manhattan has more than enough psychiatrists, but there are not enough pediatricians in the ghetto; there are so many radiologists in Los Angeles that they have to inflate their fees to keep their income above the so-called starvation level ($60,000 a year), but rural Iowa lacks enough general practitioners. Thus, what is called for is not simply more doctors, but a system of incentives to the medical schools to correct the problems of geographical and specialty maldistribution.

Talk about a capital shortage may be as misleading and nonoperational as talk about a shortage of doctors. No doubt, some capital is going to different uses than in the past—and these uses may not be in the long-range interest of the economy—but this is a problem of distribution, not of supply.[18]

Walter Heller has put forth the argument (based on Brookings, Citibank, and Data Resources studies) that the capital problems of America are not as great as cover stories in *Business Week* or editorials in the *Wall Street Journal* imply.[19] Heller shows that the ratio of business fixed investment to GNP has been rather steady since 1946, and has even climbed slightly in the last two years. Moreover, those who estimate the total capital needs of the nation for the next decade at $4 to $5 trillion are probably crisis-mongering; still, even these figures represent only 16 percent of GNP, about 1 percent over the average capital needs for the United States over the last thirty years. Heller readily admits that the U.S. rate of growth has not recently matched Germany's or Japan's, but they are still playing catch-up and Heller finds no evidence that their economies could retain their current rates of growth at our level of development and affluence. Heller also points to studies showing that much of our growth comes not from heavy investments in expensive new machines, but from advances in knowledge. Much of this is, of course, speculation. Still, we feel it seems premature to declare a capital crisis.

But one thing now seems as inevitable as death and taxes: the government will take an increasing role in the energy field. Indeed, if nuclear fusion is the wave of the future it would lead to the de facto nationalization of the U.S. energy industry. Private industry simply cannot afford the capital costs of fusion.

The funding of new energy technologies is slowly becoming the domain of the public sector because of immense costs, long gestation periods, and high risk, and because much innovation has no foreseeable short-run payoff in the marketplace.

The Delphi panel reached an early and strong consensus on the issue of government-sponsored research and development. These expenditures would continue to grow like Topsy, from $295 million in 1970 to $1.6 billion in 1985 (in 1973 dollars). Certainly energy scarcity will trigger frantic searches for new alternative energy sources and for energy-saving technologies. We can expect this effort to be massively funded by government in several ways:

- Increased research and development expenditures.

- Government incentives and support of funding by private institutional intermediaries, strengthening the position of these institutions.

- Government guarantees of price supports of industrial debt and equity offerings, which could drastically alter the normal market allocation of credit.

Effects on Income Distribution and Poverty   Poverty was a problem
in the United States before the energy crisis, and it will be a problem
no matter which energy policy the country chooses to pursue. This
is not to say that the poor must always be with us—most dire poverty has been eliminated in Scandinavia, Switzerland, Holland, Germany, New Zealand, and in other countries with market economies—
it is merely to face the fact that energy policy is a poor lever on poverty. Without inconsistency, one could fervently believe that poverty
is the largest problem in America and still support an energy policy
that did not address the question of poverty or income inequalities.
As the *Project Independence* report notes, income distribution would
not be greatly affected by any of the wide range of energy policy options available to the nation.

   Objections to higher energy prices and deregulation of energy industries because of their negative effect on the poor have some logic
in the short run but may be counterproductive in the longer term.
Clearly poor people spend a greater percentage of their income on
energy than do the wealthy. The poorest quartile spend something
like 15 percent of their total income on energy, while the wealthiest
fourth spend only about 4 percent[20] (see Exhibit 19).

   Furthermore, in addition to energy's greater importance in the
family budget, the price elasticity of demand for energy by low-in-
come groups appears to be much lower than for higher income
groups; the latter can and will cut back more on home heating,
travel, and the like. This relative disadvantage of the poor is further
compounded by the soaring costs of heating oil. Gas and electricity
pricing practices, which may be justifiable from the traditional economic efficiency standpoint, usually are such that higher volume
users pay lower average prices than lower volume users.

   In addition to these direct energy-use effects, the poor tend to
spend relatively higher percentages of their incomes on physical
goods, which also increase in price as energy costs go up. However,
to conclude from these data that higher energy prices will exacerbate

Exhibit 19
Percentage of After-Tax Income Spent on All Energy Purchases by Urban Households

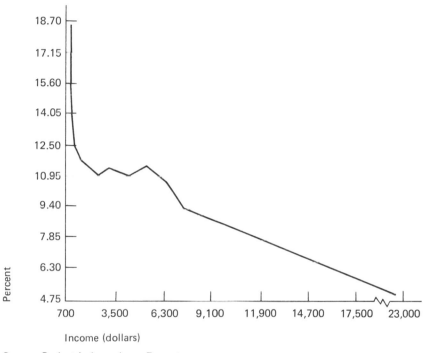

Source: Project Independence Report

the problems of poverty in America is to look at only half the
ledger.

Basically, the problem of poverty in America is closely tied to unemployment rates. The key to abolishing most poverty is to create
more and better paying jobs. Increased energy prices will lead to increased demand for labor, a rise in general wages, and an increase of
the share of gross national product going to labor as a whole. Because one aspect of unequal income distribution is the concentrated
ownership of capital, a greater income share to labor should benefit
those income groups below the richest quarter of the population.

Moreover, the most energy-intensive industries—man-made fibers,
petroleum refining, coal mining, utilities, aluminum, cement, plastics,
and paper—tend to be capital-intensive. Thus, they tend to employ
above average proportions of skilled workers. At the other end of the
energy- and capital-intensity spectrum are retail sales and many service industries that employ above average proportions of low-skilled
workers. Except for the fact that some of the latter industries, especially services, are rather income-elastic, this suggests that increasing
energy prices will not hurt lower skilled occupations relatively as
much as higher skilled occupations. Furthermore, if increased construction for new types of capital substitution as well as specific programs to meet the energy crisis take place, construction industry
demand will call for high proportions of semiskilled and unskilled
workers. One could even argue that low energy prices tend to exacerbate the problems of poverty through encouraging the substitution
of machines for the jobs of the poor.

The effects of higher energy prices on the aged are worse than on
the poor. Incomes of the aged do not tend to benefit as much from
increased employment opportunities, but older people bear higher
than average consumption costs for heating and public transportation.[21]

With the exception of the problems of the aged, the effects of
higher energy prices on income and poverty seem to balance out. In
the long run, demographic changes will probably tilt the scales in a

positive direction. An increasingly older population with fewer children per family will have higher savings and reduced need for education and welfare public services. This means that there is a greater likelihood of full employment and greater capital availability in the future. Moreover, older people, people with higher incomes, and people without children demand relatively more services than goods, and the goods they demand tend to be higher quality goods. This combination of factors bodes well for lower unemployment and energy consumption and higher incomes and life quality.

International Effects of Rising Energy Prices
Although this study of energy and social change primarily considers the domestic effects of energy availability, it is impossible to isolate the United States from world considerations. The energy crisis of 1974 was after all a short but painful lesson in how interdependent the nations and economies of the world have become. Indeed, the Delphi panel feels that in 1985 the United States will still be dependent on foreign sources for 19 percent of its total energy needs. This continued dependence on nondomestic energy (mostly oil) would lead to a 15 percent increase in foreign investments in U.S. corporations in the next decade. The panel does not look on this trend with alarm. Most panelists commented that the United States could recycle this amount of petrodollars as much-needed investment capital; some felt we could become bankers for the world, helping the Arabs place their money in solid investments; and still others felt that the long-term effect of petrodollars on the world economy will force greater stability in the international monetary system.

The economic optimism of the panel was not matched with political optimism, however. The greatest consensus reached in the entire Delphi study was the 80 percent likelihood of another Arab-Israeli war by 1980. If such a war were to occur, most of the panel think that the Arabs would try to impose another oil embargo. With these notable exceptions, the panel was basically hopeful about the effect of world political and economic actions on the United States.

Effects on the Formation of New International Cartels   By their
very nature, international cartels are hard to maintain. They tend to
be undermined sooner or later by disagreement among their members,
by the development of substitute products, or by changing political
or economic conditions. Maintaining an artificially high price through
cartel action sets in motion a succession of counterforces that sooner
or later bring the price down. The Delphi study showed half the respondents forecasting the end of the OPEC by 1980.

There is no question, however, that the less-developed countries
will in the future try to use their control over vital raw materials and
foodstuffs, including copper, bauxite, tin, iron ore, chrome ore, man-
ganese, and coffee, as leverage to get more for themselves from the
industrialized countries and to offset their own high energy and food
costs. The bauxite and natural rubber producers have already formed
organizations to discuss this, and representatives of almost a hundred
less-developed countries recently met in Dakar, Senegal, to plan a
strategy. These countries want a restructuring of the terms of world
trade in their favor and more aid in various forms from the rich
nations.

Prolonged energy scarcity would make it more likely that the OPEC
would survive and therefore that producers of other materials would
try to imitate them. On the other hand, a scarcity of energy might
also hold down the growth rates of the industrialized countries and
thus their demand for other raw materials, consequently making it
more difficult for other cartels to be formed.

But beyond this is the broader issue of relations between the rich
nations and the poor nations—the haves and have-nots. Tensions will
grow as views and policies conflict over a wide range of issues, including trade and trade policy, international investment, food, world
monetary affairs, the environment, and so on. If the United States
and the Soviet Union could achieve real détente and reduce the burden of armaments, and if then all the rich countries would give top
priority to a great partnership effort with the poor countries to pro-
pel them out of their present poverty and into successful growth,

then these tensions could lessen. Energy abundance would obviously contribute to the lessening of tensions and help the less-developed countries; energy scarcity would make the whole problem more difficult. But other factors than energy will be more important. Certainly, the rich-poor division is likely to be the most serious international problem of the last quarter of the twentieth century—much more so than the cold war or the energy crisis.

Effects on the Prospects of Military Warfare   Fewer than half of the Delphi respondents expected military warfare to follow the present economic warfare between OPEC and the consumers. (And nuclear warfare between the superpowers seems increasingly unlikely because, despite all its stupidities over the centuries, the human race has never shown signs of committing the ultimate stupidity—its self-destruction.) The present conflict between OPEC and the consumers is pushing both sides into negotiations and compromise as a matter of mutual self-interest. If energy is abundant in the years ahead, obviously there is no issue. If it is scarce, a joint effort to find solutions makes sense for all concerned; confrontation does not.

   If peace is more assured in the years ahead, gradually more of the world's resources will be available for the primary problem—developing the poor countries. Clearly, a separate study of this issue is needed. Indeed, a main purpose of the second USC Twenty-Year Forecast is to explore whether and how the world's food resources would be used to help these countries, and with what effects.

Effects on the Formation of International and Supranational Organizations   What effect will energy scarcity have on the formation and functioning of international organizations (in which sovereign states cooperate) and supranational bodies (to which they surrender some sovereignty)?

   It is difficult to isolate the energy influences here because historic world forces are pushing the world inexorably toward more economic integration. This trend is not going to be greatly reversed by energy developments. The historic forces are technology, investment, trade, and a growing recognition that such world problems as food, energy, population growth, inflation, and the environment are indivisible. Either the human race will find collective solutions to these problems, or no solutions will be found and all humanity will suffer. This is why today we have the Organization for Economic Cooperation and Development, the Geneva Agreement on Tariffs and Trade, the World Health Organization, the Organization of American States, the World Bank, the European Common Market, the World Population Conference, the World Food Conference, the United Nations Environmental Council, and many other bodies.

The nation-state is gradually becoming obsolete for some functions, just as the feudal system became obsolete in Europe at the end of the Middle Ages—and for the same reasons. Although our generation or even the next will not see world government, we will see the continued erosion of national sovereignty (though not its complete surrender), the strengthening of existing supranational bodies like the Common Market, and the creation of new international organizations, of which the International Energy Agency is only the latest. In the context of world history, energy developments will have only a marginal effect.

The consensus of the Delphi panel was that several kinds of supranational groups are likely to be formed in coming years:

- Oil consumer organization

- World Food Bank

- Regional blocs around powerful neighbors

- Ocean resources management organization

- Strengthened International Monetary Fund or IMF-type organization to recycle oil funds

- Raw materials cartels for such commodities as tin, sugar, bauxite, and iron

The panel felt, however, that the importance of energy availability as a factor in the forming of such organizations was easily overstated. On a scale from 1 (energy is the central factor) to 10 (energy not a factor at all) the median estimate of the panel of the importance of energy was 6.

Effects on Specialization and Dependence For centuries as technology has developed and trade and investment have expanded, nations have tended to specialize more and more and to become increasingly interdependent. No nation can live and prosper alone in the modern world, not even the United States. What effect will energy abundance or energy scarcity have on this?

Higher cost energy would obviously increase the dependence of those who lack it on those who have it. Presumably, deficient nations would also be trying to develop new sources of energy behind protective barriers. This protectionism would have an adverse effect on international trade and balances of payments and would push more countries into self-sufficiency in other products besides energy. Scarcity breeds controls, and controls mean less specialization and interdependence.

On the other hand, the effect of scarcity of energy on the United States economy could lead toward some quite healthy specialization in those things we do well—agriculture, high technology, services, and knowledge industries—and leave to others with more abundant energy sources the making of such things as aluminum and mass-produced goods. Numerous opportunities here have not been tapped. For example, resource-exporting nations have a tremendous demand for educated workers but they lack the domestic capability of educating and training great numbers of their citizens. Of all the nations in the world, only one has a fully developed educational and training system. That one country, the United States, also has a severe overcapacity in this field. The United States could recycle millions of petrodollars, bauxite dollars, or tin dollars by making education one of its largest export industries. This could be done by charging foreign students tuition at American schools and universities that covered the full cost of their education, plus a markup. At the present time U.S. taxpayers subsidize foreign students. In the future, foreign students could not only pay for what they receive but they could also help to underwrite the cost of the education of American students. The problem here is not one of further investment, it is one of marketing and managing.

Social Effects of Rising Energy Prices

The United States is undergoing a period of rapid and far-reaching social change. Attitudes about sex roles, family, divorce, drugs, dress, work, religion, and the environment are in a transitional state—changing too fast for some and not fast enough to suit the tastes of others. But what are the causes of these changes in attitudes and behaviors? Clearly, when it comes to identifying causation, the social sciences are at a primitive stage in their development.

Still, it at least seems safe to say that the role of energy in social change has often been overstated in the last three years. For example, people who should have known better were unabashedly predicting that higher energy prices would lead to the following changes in society:

- A massive middle-class resettlement of the central cities

- A wholesale switch from the private auto to public transportation

- A wide-scale substitution of communications for transportation

Several apparent fallacies led to this line of reasoning. First, there was the mistaken notion that energy was a kind of master force in determining where people live, how they live, and what they think. Indeed, as history shows, the use of various energy forms and technologies is a cultural choice. Energy, then, follows culture as much as if not more than culture follows energy. Second, there was the mistaken notion that because gas lines were running around the block energy was about the only major influence on people's thinking. In

fact, Watergate, international peace, inflation, taxation, food shortages, health and safety, corporate, political, and union shenanigans,
good schools for the kids, and job- and leisure-satisfaction were all
major variables affecting the attitudes of the average American citizen. Energy was important, but it was not the only thing on Joe Citizen's mind by a long shot. Third, there was the mistaken notion that
people will alter their behavior overnight when faced with a crisis. In
fact, people change very slowly. To begin, they wait to see if the
crisis is real or if it will pass. If it does not pass, they weigh the costs
of change against preserving the status quo. Only if the costs of present behaviors are prohibitively high will they change—and then they
will not change radically, but just enough to remove the source of
pain.

Then how could it be expected that the middle class would return
to the central cities because the cost of gasoline doubled or even
quadrupled? In Europe, where the relative cost of gas and car ownership is perhaps three or four times what it is in the United States, the
familiar suburban sprawl is as prevalent as in this country. The fact is
that the middle class wants to get away from the poverty, congestion,
crime, taxes, and pollution of the central cities—and it is willing to
pay the price of transportation to have its dream half-acre in suburbia. Moreover, the cost of escape is not yet very high nor does it
promise to become prohibitively high in the next decade. B. Bruce-
Briggs writes that if the price of gasoline had risen at the rate of all
other prices relative to median family income since 1955, it would
cost 80 cents a gallon today.[22] Thus, gas is still a bargain in the eyes
of the average American—and if his European counterpart is any in-
dication, it will still be a bargain at $2 a gallon if it helps him to get
away from the rotting core of the city.

Moreover, the commuter does not think only in terms of the cost
of gasoline. He also values his time. Using this measure, it has gotten
increasingly cheap to live in the suburbs. The effective radius of urban
areas (the distance one can travel from the city center in 30 minutes)
has increased tenfold since 1890. In 1890, the effective radius on

foot or horseback was 2 miles. With the advent of public transit, the radius increased to 8 miles in 1920. In 1950, the car could take the commuter 11 miles in 30 minutes. The completion of major freeway systems allowed the commuter to stretch his 30 minutes over 20 to 24 miles in the 1970s.[23] Thus, with the exception of the price of gas, all the leading trends point to urban spread and suburbanization—at least they do not portend retreat to the city's core. Consequently, the Delphi panel forecasts only a very slight reverse migration of the middle class to the central cities as the result of energy scarcity.

Moreover, the suburban commuter is not likely to be whisked into his central-city job aboard either some futuristic form of mass transportation or even on a plain old bus. He values his freedom, time, and flexibility too much to make such a change. The failure of San Francisco's BART to attract passengers in what must be America's second most ideal location (after New York) for a rapid transit system is evidence that it is going to take more than just high gas prices to make public transportation attractive. The Delphi panel injected a note of cold realism in this area: they forecast that the percentage of all commuter miles to work in private cars would drop to only 81% in 1985 (from 85% in 1975).

One of the favorite forecasts of futurists is that transportation will increasingly be traded off in favor of communications. In plain English, this means that instead of driving to work, school, or the doctor, one would simply tune in the two-way television-cum-computer in one's living room and "interact" (as the engineers say). There are several practical problems with this Buck Rogers view of the world. First, the hardware involved is terribly expensive. It would cost many billions of dollars to wire America with two-way cable televisions. Second, few people other than futurist engineers need or want a computer terminal in their home. Third and most significant, human contact is one of the most important and satisfying parts of work and school experiences and of doctor-patient relationships. The communications revolution then would not only require more capital than is available in the next decade, it would also require a change in human nature. No doubt the communications revolution will continue, but it is unlikely to be as dramatic a shift as some futurists wish.

The thinking behind the mass-transit and mass-communications forecasts highlights two misconceptions on the part of the engineering mind: (1) that big technology is the solution to all human problems; and (2) that because a technology is available or feasible it will or should be used. These misconceptions run throughout the mainstream of thought concerning the energy situation and skew forecasts unrealistically in the direction of early technological solutions to the problem. Somehow the costs of new technology and the costs of depreciation of the old get lost in the enthusiasm for big, new, shiny gadgetry.

Changing Expectations and Values All this is not to say that energy scarcity will have no effect on society or that new technologies will not alter our lives. But in the short run the effects of higher energy prices will be rather subtle, indirect, and individualized. To the extent that energy scarcity reinforces other major social trends, it will influence the values, expectations, and behaviors of Americans. But acting alone or running counter to stronger forces, energy is unlikely to have a great degree of short-term social influence.

In concert with several other important factors, energy scarcity might have some profoundly negative second-order (unanticipated) consequences. For example, since the time of de Tocqueville's travels to America in the 1840s, foreign observers have characterized Americans as optimistic about the future. The expectations of the average citizen have always been that tomorrow will be better than today. Each American has felt that in the future he or she will be richer, happier, and better situated socially. Among immigrants, the dream was often deferred for a generation: parents felt that it was too late for them to make it in American society, but little Chester or Charlotte would go to Harvard. Indeed, among second- and third-generation ethnic Americans, success is most often measured by "doing better than your parents." For all social classes, this faith in the

future led to what is called "deferred gratification"—the postponing
of current consumption in favor of an investment leading to even
greater satisfaction in the future. (For example, one would be willing
to work ten years on an auto assembly line to accumulate the capital
needed to open a gas station.) Deferred gratification is, of course, the
essence of the Protestant ethic. Those who defer save, and saving is
good for the economy as well as for the soul.

A few years ago, something unusual began to happen in America.
The country seemed to lose its confidence about the future. In the
public context, Americans used to believe that any problem could be
solved by Yankee ingenuity, from winning the West to putting a man
on the moon. Lately, however, the best efforts of Americans have
failed to make much headway against such problems as racial conflict, poverty, and pollution. This shook our national confidence. The
blows might have been glancing had they not been followed so closely by the loss of the Vietnam war and the Watergate revelations.

On the personal level, nostalgia replaced the future optimism of the
average American. A recent survey of attitudes found that middle-
class Americans were scaling down their expectations about housing
in the future.[24] Gone were the newlyweds' dreams of a large single-
family dwelling in a wealthy neighborhood. Instead there was the
realistic vision of a small townhouse in an unsafe neighborhood. According to preliminary results from this study and from other evidence from pollsters, Americans apparently do not feel that their
standard of living will improve as it has in the past.

During the energy crisis, public opinion polls found a startling drop
in expectations about the future, in faith in major institutions, in confidence that the quality of life is improving, that government can or
will solve problems, that people can make a difference in politics,
and that the position of the poor will improve relative to the position
of the rich. Of course, it was not simply that energy prices were rising that cast this pervasive gloom over the American public. Gas lines
in addition to Watergate, crime, inflation, and a host of other real or
perceived ills were obviously just too much for even Joe Citizen to
take in his normally sanguine way.

The average American saw quite clearly, moreover, that rising energy prices were eroding the economic growth on which his optimism was premised. The American dream is not one of redistribution of the economic pie; rather it is historically based on a growing pie with bigger pieces for everyone. A slowing of economic growth—of which rising energy prices were the clearest indicator to the average American—was a signal that his share of the action would not be expanding.

In a stationary economy there are only two options: accepting the status quo of relative inequality, or redistribution. America has not recently been faced with such a politically explosive choice. If growth does slow, the painfully difficult course of redistribution may be inevitable. Appeals to Joe and Josephine Citizen and their peers to work harder will fall on deaf ears if they see little or no reward for their effort. The potential for radical or populist political activity would be heightened by such a state of affairs. Less dramatic, but in the long run possibly destructive of the economic system, would be the simple shift from deferred gratification to instant consumption as the new American ethic. People who feel they have no future act in ways that have been traditionally considered self-destructive and antisocial in America.

Poor blacks and other members of what Moynihan calls the "under-class" exhibit this kind of behavior. Quite realistically, members of the under-class view their futures as extensions of their miserable presents. Indeed, if one has ten dollars in one's pocket, the future may appear worse than the present. The sensible thing then is to "grab all the gusto" one can in the present. It is not surprising, then, to see some impoverished blacks drinking expensive Scotch (blacks drink half of the Scotch consumed in the United States), wearing expensive clothes, taking drugs, and behaving in a generally happy-go-lucky manner. Saving and planning for the future have little part in such a life-style, and as a consequence such things as family stability and conscientious work habits are seldom fostered.

Is this the future cultural paradigm for America? Certainly, constantly falling expectations might be expected to erode the propensity to save and cause even the most upstanding citizens to engage in frenetic consumption. Indeed, paralleling the energy crisis, America underwent one of its most severe savings droughts. Money in savings and loans for new home construction all but dried up. There was even a bit of panic buying a la Latin America as consumers tried to stay ahead of inflation. In the midst of the energy crisis, it looked as though this country was going to hell in an oil barrel.

Interestingly, energy prices have continued to climb, but according to a poll by Daniel Yankelovich in May 1975 Americans are beginning to regain some confidence in the future.[25] Feelings about inflation, the recession, and social resentment all seemed to have turned around within the space of a year. At the same time, the University of Michigan's Survey Research Center found consumer confidence growing. Apparently, scarce energy is not enough to affect the thinking of Americans permanently.

However, the energy situation does appear to have changed one important attitude of the American consumer. According to some observers, it would seem that Americans are becoming quality conscious. The age of conspicuous consumption may be nearing an end. If this is so, and it is too early to tell with certainty, then this would do much to offset the problem of the shrinking pie. Under the old growth assumption, a good American was a conspicuous consumer, constantly trading up for a bigger car, a fancier stereo, and a newer television—one with an energy-wasting gadget to make the picture appear the moment the set is turned on. Under the traditional assumptions, to tell Joe Citizen he could not have these things was to invite a populist or some other kind of radical reaction. However, if the values of America are changing and the good American is becoming a careful consumer worried more about quality than quantity, more about durability than flashiness, more about energy saving than gadgetry, Joe Citizen can find satisfaction in a more frugal environment.

No one knows if this change in values has occurred. Certainly it has affected the upper middle class. In 1972, bikes outsold new cars. The sale of vegetable seeds skyrocketed. Small cars outsold big cars. But the upper middle class is really not that important: they have been buying Volkswagens for twenty years and not convincing their working-class compatriots a whit that durability and economy were to be valued. It is when steelworkers start buying Honda Civics that one will know a major shift in values has occurred.

The zero-energy-growth scenario of the Ford Foundation's *Time to Choose* offers an interesting case study in this regard. The report projected a situation in which existing levels of energy usage grow at a much slower rate and eventually stabilize because of a trend toward preference for "real" values. The scenario seems to assume, among other things, a growing disenchantment with material progress and with the idea that higher and higher levels of consumption are the proper measure of the quality of life. If there are such things as "real" as opposed to "artificial" values—that is, if "real" values are something other than my preferences, there are few signs of movement toward them among any group but upper-middle-class intellectuals.

The Delphi panel feels that the price of energy will have to go much higher than it has for trends in personal consumption to change. They estimate, for example, that the cost of energy would have to increase 45 percent to cause consumers to invest substantially in energy-saving home improvements. Similarly, they forecast that it will be some time before consumers will be willing to make the trade-off in home appliances with higher initial purchase prices to have lower annual operating costs. The panel estimates that the higher initial price would have to be amortized in three years through savings in operating costs to induce substantial numbers of consumers to buy such energy-saving appliances.

The middle and working classes are not yet quality- and energy-conscious. But the cost of energy is trending in such a way that it is possible to see the day when Joe Citizen will count his kilowatts—that day, however, is still around the corner.

In short, it is conceivable that the way people feel—the kind of life-styles they value—will be more important than technological changes in determining future energy needs and policies. Our Delphi panel suggested, for example, that life-styles (for example, family structure) will not significantly be affected by energy shortages. Institutional changes, though we often place great stress on them, may be more a function than a determinant of cultural styles and values. Changes in cultural values, as Bertrand de Jouvenel reminds us, are notoriously difficult, if not impossible, to predict with any precision (witness the rapidly outdated social projections produced in the 1950s and '60s).[26]

We know there will be changes in values, and we know these will be important—we just do not know which direction the change will be in or what will cause the change!

Effects on Political Participation Nevertheless, there do seem to be signs that we can expect some growth in conservationist values and consequently an increased scrutiny of public and private policy-making processes by ecology-minded groups. This movement is closely associated with consumerism and possibly related to perceptions that oil companies have been allowed to accumulate excessive profits and thereby to benefit from the public's energy misfortunes. (As we have seen, it might also be related to an increased difficulty in the public's ability to satisfy personal needs.) Whatever the cause, our Delphi panel strongly agreed that energy policy will be formulated in a heightened democratic environment: 70 percent of the panel predicted increased public participation, while 24 percent believed that it would remain essentially level; only 5 percent predicted a decrease.

The general conclusion is quite significant, because the situation could well have been otherwise. It might reasonably have been argued that energy uses and impacts are so pervasive and diverse that it would be extremely difficult to organize viable political factions around any particular energy issue. Furthermore, it is easily conceivable that the public could be pictured as having become so cynical and alienated from politics in recent years that its level of participation might decline if shortages make clearer to individuals that they are losing control over their own destinies. Our panelists disagree. They expect activism.

The panel's conclusions about political participation are significant
for yet another reason. They suggest that the important transitions in
values within our culture may relate only indirectly to substantive
ways in which energy will be secured and used. Policy makers probably should not concern themselves extensively with predicting tastes
and values that may be developing independently from changes in
the energy situation. At the present time there simply do not seem to
be solid bases for such projections.[27] But what does appear to be important are the procedures and values within which future allocative
choices will be made—that is, the perceived fairness of the ground
rules and the fairness of the resultant allocative decisions. These of
course are classic political issues, and the problems are consistently
present in the American political arena. They are structural. In effect,
our panel is warning policy makers not to become overly fascinated
with novelties in the emergent energy situation, not to be enamored
with possibilities that energy policies will have to be determined in
the context of the essentially mysterious: new values, new tastes,
new institutions, and new forms of technology. These factors undoubtedly will intrude, but the novel should not be allowed to mask
the perennial. Americans habitually frame their political choices within the concern for freedom, equality, and fair process (accessibility of
all major groups to the process in which choices are made). These
values also will constitute the context for determining future policies
in the energy field. Indeed, our panel argues that this context may
well be the dominant consideration in light of the likelihood of
heightened political awareness and participation.

**Effects of Energy Availability on the Resilience of American Institu-
tions** Critics of Western culture have traditionally observed that
mobility is high within the Western hierarchy of values. Our very
sense of freedom, they observe, is related to an ability to move
around, to have a large number of choices, not to feel constrained.
Following this logic, a period of constrained expectations and of restricted physical movement must be regarded as possibly fatal to
American institutions as we have known them. One critic, Jurgen

Moultman, argues that we already have had sufficient experience
with restricted mobility to know what to expect.[28] Although the urban environment in large part has assumed easy movement, he says,
it has also encouraged a perception that movement is difficult and
that people are constrained. The result is a significant change in cultural values. Values have emerged that emphasize "inner space," that
suggest withdrawal into a more individualistic, personal sphere. But,
paradoxically, these also give rise to radical movements aimed at restructuring the frustrating, constraining environment. In short, Moultman associates restricted mobility with both increased individualism
and with episodic radical activism. Restricted mobility, in his view,
will introduce a period of troubles for American institutions, particularly because the traditional values that undergird these institutions
will be eroding.

Our Delphi panelists project a different picture: an American society that will be amazingly resilient in relation to energy availability.
In the event of prolonged energy shortages, the panel projects important adjustments in land use, the decentralization of governmental
and commercial activities, and the forging of new social middlemen
(arbitration-mediation) functions. But these adjustments are all well
within the bounds of traditional American institutions. Likewise, the
panelists believe that there are whole areas of American life that pro-
ceed in ways that are relatively independent of changes in energy
availability—family structure, for example. They do not view energy
as the central factor in maintaining the social fabric, and they even
indicate that it may not even be among the most important.

Although most shortages are interlinked, a food shortage, for example, could be expected to encourage far higher organizational,
social, and cultural dissonance than an energy shortage. Food affects
a more basic needs level than does energy, and food shortages would
quickly increase citizen dissatisfaction with government and with private corporate structures. Against this background, the panelists' argument that energy shortages would not so vitally affect the social order
becomes significant. Contrary to beliefs held by many critics, mobil-

ity and the availability of a broad range of choice do not appear to be
the primary values, at least in the sense that their curtailment (within
the range projected for the possible future shortages) would create a
revolutionary situation.

The panelists suggest that any extended period of energy shortage
will promote a high level of readjustment In government and corporate activities as well as high levels of citizen participation. This will
be a period in which institutions will experience what will internally
appear to be profound changes (like major forms of bureaucratic re-
organization), but in the long term these changes clearly will be interpreted as a healthy reenergizing of the social fabric. In short, the
changes projected do not appear to be fundamental. They are not on
the order of catastrophe or of a reshaping of government systems.

Our panel strongly agreed about the likelihood of such a period of
restructuring, but there was an impressive level of disagreement concerning the specific character of the transitions involved. The dissensus is noteworthy because at least it ought to qualify any certainty
we might have about predicting social and political trends. More important, the dissensus reminds us that in the social and political
sphere prediction is thoroughly enmeshed in social theory, and there
is little agreement here. What agreement there is, therefore, is significant; and the agreement is by and large optimistic. The energy problem is viewed as a turning point, but not a devastating one. Democratic institutions will be capable of making the necessary adjustments without serious decline.

Effects of Alternative Government Policies In an attempt to identify
the long-range political consequences of energy scarcity, the Delphi
study examined two possible modes of governmental response: market pricing and nonmarket regulation (such as allocation and controls).

According to the panel, energy scarcity can be expected to increase
society's reliance on public and private bureaucracies regardless of
whether market pricing or government regulations are used to deal

with the scarcity. This trend will somewhat encourage the emergence
of social ombudsmen—mini Ralph Naders—to assist the public in dealing with the increasingly bureaucratized institutions. This development seems likely to increase the level of conflict between individuals (or groups) and social institutions for several reasons. First, such
ombudsmen will be operating in an atmosphere of heightened political awareness. Second, the ombudsmen will raise the level of public
awareness about its rights when dealing with the bureaucracy, thereby increasing the demands on—and the potential for conflict with—
the bureaucracy. In short, energy scarcity portends greater dissatisfaction with the performance of social institutions.

However, significant differences between market pricing and government regulation scenarios are also perceived by the panelists. Government regulations, for example, are viewed as a fairer method of
allocating the burdens of energy scarcity. Reliance on market-pricing
mechanisms, in contrast, is considered to lead to significantly lower
levels of bureaucratization. Consequently, market pricing would result in less reliance on middlemen.

Perhaps more significant is the agreement of the panelists that
greater bureaucratization will significantly limit organizational and
individual flexibility (freedom) to respond to energy-imposed constraints. But freedom has not been the only star in the constellation
of American values. Concepts of equality and fairness have often
equaled and sometimes eclipsed freedom in importance. And some
of the appeal of government regulation lies in its treatment of these
values. Thus, regulation is perceived as fairer than market pricing because it offers the promise of limiting the transfer of wealth from energy consumers to energy producers, that is, it is more likely to produce equal treatment than would the free market. In addition, it is
fairer in that the results are dictated by political forces (one man, one
vote) rather than economic forces. Daniel Bell lauds this development: "Today . . . there is a visible change from market to nonmarket political decision making. The market disperses responsibility:
the political center is visible, the question of who gains and loses is

clear, and government becomes a cockpit."[29] That government has
become a "cockpit" of American energy policy since the crisis is
clear. That the resulting constraints can be viewed as promoting equality and fairness is much less clear, and herein lies the danger. If these
limits on the freedom of business firms, for example, to adapt to energy scarcity lead to reduced performance, the public is likely to become even more dissatisfied with business and demand more controls. The results would make even the Mad Hatter smile.

Thus, energy scarcity is likely to focus the political debate on the
underlying tension between the values of freedom, equality, and fairness. This suggests that the issues will be debated in traditional politi-
cal-morality terms. Though this debate will probably increase societal
feelings of uncertainty, the prospect of reexamining basic social
values within a democratic framework must be viewed as a process
fundamental to the continued health of society.

But the beneficial effects of the process should not blind us to the
substantial differences that flow from reliance on government regulation and from market pricing. For some questions, our panelists see
the social trade-off as follows: freedom is reduced to increase equality
and fairness. But in answering other questions, the panel seems to
recognize that these values are not entirely inconsistent. They feel,
for example, that the unequal income distribution effects of the market pricing system can be offset by adjustments in government taxation and transfer policies. Such adjustments could preserve opera-
tional flexibility and simultaneously mitigate the objection that market pricing results in unequal, unfair treatment of consumers. The
public perception of fair treatment could also alleviate the political
strains inherent in an energy-scarce environment.

Other adjustments could lead to a similar increase of public confidence in the ability of American social institutions to respond effectively to pressing problems. Tightening of campaign finance laws, for
example, could decrease the probability that the entrenched economic interests of energy producers would unfairly pervert the political processes for their further profit. And if the public perceives the

political process as a fair method of resolving such issues, it is less
likely to demand radical changes in our political and economic institutions.

In short, the panel indicates that neither governmental regulation
nor market pricing is a panacea for an energy-scarce economy. Each
has inherent problems and limitations. But policy adjustments can be
made to offset the difficulties of market pricing—if the difficulties
are recognized in time.

Summary: Toward the Year 1985

The next decade will be marked by higher energy prices, increased
governmental activity in the marketplace, and an accelerated rate of
substitutions among types of goods and among industrial processes.
The following is a consensus picture of the next ten years compiled
from the Delphi findings and the conclusions of task forces based on
their own analyses and review of the literature:

- Global catastrophes are unlikely—there is little chance of an oil war
  or worldwide depression.

- More effort (money, manpower, and energy) will be required to extract each unit of energy.

- A smaller fraction of U.S. productive capacity will turn out mass-
  produced consumer goods; old style burgeoning of affluence will
  level off.

- The period will be unstable and transitional for the economic, political, social, and technological orders. Substitutions and temporary
  measures will proliferate.

- In the United States, energy-intensive activities and industrial processes will begin to be replaced by less energy-intensive ones.

- Social costs will be paid more promptly, rather than leaving them for
  future generations to pay. For example, pollution costs will be inter-

nalized in costs of products, land spoiled by mining will be more quickly restored.

- Energy research and capital investment will increase disproportionately, leaving less money for other types of research and investment.

- Rates of unemployment will drop.

- There will be a gradual shift to smaller families, smaller cars, smaller homes, less planned obsolescence and waste, and a little less comfort in the home, car, and at work.

- Such close-at-hand neighborhood activities as recreation, work, education, politics, and commerce (shopping) will increase.

- Energy will have little effect on family styles, use of private cars. mass transit systems, substitution of communications for transportation, etc.

- Individual responses to energy scarcity (such as use of bicycles, heating homes with individual solar units, growing vegetable gardens, producing backyard methane) will increase slightly.

- There is a high probability that OPEC will deteriorate to the point where it is no longer able to control petroleum prices.

- The rates of economic growth, energy use, and inflation will drop slightly.

- No strong national energy policy will probably be adopted. Rather there will be a piecemeal approach incorporating several features:

  Price supports for domestic producers

  Accelerated support for fusion programs

  Tax on "excessive" consumption

  Development of solar, geothermal, methane, and other secondary sources

Heavy reliance on research and development

Increase in domestic production of oil, gas, uranium, and coal

Reduction of environmental standards

In short, because such fossil fuels as petroleum (and natural gas to a lesser extent) will still be available during the next decade, few severe social or economic dislocations are likely. Higher prices will force conservation, substitution, and some sacrifice, but this process will be gradual and manageable, although at times a bit unpleasant and hard on the pocketbook.

What is crucial is not what will actually happen during the 1975-1985 period as the consequence of higher energy prices, but what will happen in the subsequent decades *as the result of choices made during this time.* Beginning in about 1990 to 2000, there is little that can be forecasted with certainty. The future, either one of scarcity or one of abundance, depends on the choices being made now and during the next ten years.

4. The Long-Term Future: Realizing the Opportunities of Energy Options

Forecasting the world of 1994 involves much more than projecting the trends at hand or even reciting the possibilities ahead. That future will be determined in large part by our considering and choosing values, examining and deciding among alternatives, exercising great will and perseverance, and searching for the leadership that will assemble and catalyze the proper resources to construct a chosen future.

Glenn T. Seaborg
Nobel Prize Winner, Chemistry

Between 1940 when Robert Millikan wrote the words that introduce the first chapter of this study and 1974 when Glenn Seaborg wrote the lines above, a great change in attitude apparently occurred in the American scientific community. The Millikan quotation expresses the once widely held faith that, left to their own judgments and devices, scientists and technologists would provide the necessary means for the improvement of society. Although Seaborg shares Millikan's optimism about the ability of science and technology to deliver almost anything mankind orders, he differs in that he feels that the most difficult challenge facing the human race is to decide *what* to order. In the last three decades social and political issues have apparently assumed preeminence over the scientific and technological.

In the long term, Western societies are relatively free to choose whatever future they desire. The extreme choices appear clear:

Growth	vs	no growth
Freedom	vs	equality
Equality	vs	efficiency
Equality	vs	quality
Employment	vs	inflation
Centralization	vs	decentralization
Open society	vs	controlled society
Humanism	vs	economic efficiency
Jobs	vs	environmental soundness
Energy production	vs	quality of life

A trade-off mentality has, unfortunately, taken hold in Western societies. (We say unfortunately because a trade-off situation is by definition a zero-sum game. Consequently, policy changes are viewed as always entailing some winners and some losers.) As early as the 1950s, Harrison Brown was asking how much freedom would have to be sacrificed in order to alter the trends that threaten the existence of advanced, pluralistic societies. Brown wrote:

Indeed, when we examine all the foreseeable difficulties which threaten the survival of industrial civilizations it is difficult to see how the achievement of stability and the maintenance of individual liberty can be made compatible.[1]

In this view—perhaps now the prevalent view of the 1970s—the trade-off is between the Scylla of resource depletion and the Charybdis of centralized planning and control. Unlike Odysseus, however, modern societies may have a third option—indeed, the most desirable options probably lie not at the extremes, but in policies designed to permit the simultaneous pursuit of apparently contradictory goals. For example, the challenge of the future may be to invent policies that promote both liberty and equality, policies that are both labor-intensive and environmentally sound, and technologies that are both productive and energy-efficient. Later in this chapter we offer some ideas about how such policies might be identified and encouraged. For the moment, let us ask if it is possible that market mechanisms can be set to work both to preserve freedom and to conserve resources? Under one scenario, individual and corporate planning could make the tough and essentially unprogrammable resource allocation decisions for society. But would this process serve the public interest? Recent West German experience indicates that it might. The energy crisis has affected the German economy less than any developed oil-importing country. Germans have an enviable record of energy conservation (demand fell 10 percent in 1974), which was achieved not through government planning or controls, but by letting the price of energy rise to the market-clearing price (which now turns out to be the lowest in Europe).

Could America do the same? The major obstacle in this country is political: one political party favors increased industrial competition but also wants artificially controlled energy prices, while the other party favors industrial concentration but with market-set prices. Unless this contradiction is resolved, America appears destined to remain impaled on the horns of painful trade-offs.

There are several other obstacles to achieving an adequate supply of energy in the 1990s through competition and free market mechanisms. First, as Charles Berg has recently written, American industry did not respond to the potential benefits of conserving energy in the past, even when it was economically efficient to do so.[2] And nothing has really changed to make the country believe that rising energy prices will suddenly make concentrated industries into entrepreneurial paradigms. Apparently, businessmen do not always respond to free market opportunities for innovation or profit. This behavior seems to have its genesis in a growing corporate inertia characterized by tradition-bound thinking, a crippling sense of security, and a lack of incentive for innovation and change. Second, private decision makers appear to be unaware of the full range of alternatives open to their institutions and of the costs and benefits of change.

Both these obstacles may be overcome by future events. The rising price of natural resources, the low standing of business in the public eye, threats of further government controls and nationalization, increased foreign competition, and the injection of young blood in corporate boardrooms may finally shake American business out of its lethargy of the last decade. And the rediscovery by the current administration of antitrust laws and the concept that competition is more effective than regulatory agencies might also help to restore the entrepreneurial spirit to big business.

Most important, business leaders may begin to respond responsibly and innovatively if they are made more aware of the extremely broad range of options that are readily available to them and of the long-term consequences for their companies and the economic system of each of these options.

American industry is beginning to recognize that future energy choices will neither be simple nor black and white. For example, the choice is not between the Ford Foundation's "conserve at all costs" and Mobil Oil's "produce at all costs." In fact, at least ten policy options for securing an adequate supply of energy can be identified— and pursuing any one or set of these does not foreclose the concurrent or subsequent pursuit of the others (see Exhibit 20).[3] What becomes clear from analyzing this list of options is that the energy problem has no single dramatic solution; only a congeries of actions on both the supply and demand sides of the equation will permit the nation to achieve both an adequate amount of energy and a high quality of life.

What follows in this chapter is an identification of several policies that would probably lead to the realization of these two goals. Some of these options have been rejected in the past because of inertia or short-term thinking on the part of public and private decision makers. They deserve rethinking, we believe. None of these policies would be expected to bear full fruit for a decade or possibly even for twenty or thirty years. Nevertheless, each of these policies would have to be initiated soon if they are to be ready in time for the inevitable depletion of the petroleum under the sands of Arabia.

Higher Energy Prices
Higher prices are the sine qua non of achieving both an increased supply of and decreased demand for energy. Whether these high prices are achieved through market-setting means (the preferable way) or through government taxation, the long-term results might be the same:

- Pressure on the OPEC cartel

- Slower depletion of natural resources

- Increased industrial efficiency in the use of energy

- Decreased environmental pollution (particularly if environmental costs are internalized in the price of energy)

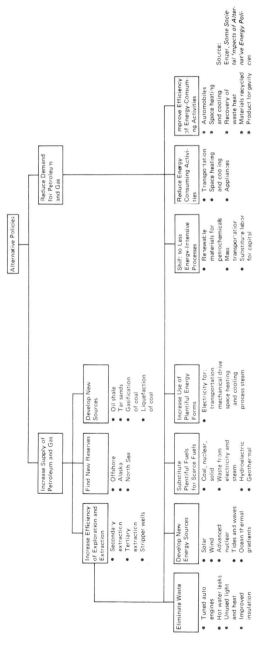

Exhibit 20
Relevance Tree Showing Alternative Means of Providing an Adequate Energy Supply by 1995

- Improvement in the quality and durability of goods

- Increased opportunity for craftsmanship

- The development of clean, renewable, alternative sources of energy

- More centralized life-styles—less commuting and chauffeuring, for example

- More decentralized economic decision making

- Less government bureaucracy and more individual freedom

With the exception of a short-term increase in inflation and adverse effects on the poor, higher energy prices promise long-term improvements in the quality of life. Moreover, Kenneth Boulding argues that to achieve these future improvements will require economizing in the present:

One of the less recognized principles of economics is that, if the price structure is going to change in the future, there is a lot to be said for anticipating this change, simply because this will promote decisions which will prepare for the future. If something is cheap now but is going to be expensive later on, there is a lot to be said for making it expensive now, and this will force technological change in the direction of economizing it. If things are "too cheap," they will not be sufficiently economized. In quieter times the best way to do this is through the tax system, by taxing things that are likely to be scarce in the future, so that it pays to start economizing them now. In regard to oil, the Arabs have now done this for us through their joyful discovery of the pleasures of monopoly. The rest of us, however, should not be too ungrateful to them, even though they are in effect imposing the taxes and enjoying the revenue from them. They may have done us a good turn without quite intending it. They have forced us to think about the rising costs of energy right now, when there is perhaps time to do something about it, whereas without this crisis we might have floated happily on an illusory tide of cheap energy until, say, 1990, when it might be too late to do anything about it.[4]

The Organization for Economic Cooperation and Development projects that at the continued real price of $11 a barrel, the United States would become self-sufficient in oil by 1985. The OECD researchers feel that this price would lead to a 114 percent increase in U.S. oil production while at the same time depressing demand. The MIT energy study group predicts that prices might have to remain as high as $13 a barrel for American self-sufficiency, but these more realistic forecasts are nevertheless consistent with the OECD message that demand for energy is elastic—that is, the market will work if we let it.[5]

One of the most important aspects of a rise in energy prices would be the eventual deterioration of the power of OPEC through forcing reductions in production and other difficult problems of allocation, and making alternative sources more attractive. This is an important consequence; in the long run, the United States cannot continue to run the risk of an Arab takeover of key sectors of the economy, of continued high inflation, or of a chronic balance of payments deficit. A breakup or defusing of the cartel, then, is essential for American policy.

In a paper commissioned for this study, Morley English demonstrates how it will be impossible for the OPEC to continue for many years in their monopolistic position, particularly at current prices.[6] Indeed, in February 1976, the Iranians began selling oil below the official OPEC price, indicating that cartel discipline—as had been predicted—would be hard to enforce in the long run. (For a summary of why the price of oil and energy might drop again in the long run, see the "Ultimate Abundance?" section in this chapter.) The Delphi panel expects the cartel to have collapsed by 1985, with a consequent drop in the international price of a barrel of crude oil to $7.70 (in constant 1973 dollars). By 1995, the panel sees the price climbing back up to $10, reflecting the inevitable depletion of even the vast Middle East reserves. For the reason offered by Boulding, even if the price of oil should drop in the next decade as the result of an OPEC collapse, the U.S. government would no doubt want to keep the price high through additional taxation.

Indeed, Harvard Business School's Robert Stobaugh argues that an additional 50 cents a gallon tax should be placed on gasoline now, and kept on.[7] Not only would the higher U.S. price weaken the cartel, the $40 billion raised in federal taxes could be used to offset the unequal economic effects of the higher prices and thus bring liberals in Congress to favor the position of higher energy prices.

In policy terms, the most important role for the federal government in establishing energy prices is probably to develop a constant taxation plan that keeps the price high. Promotional pricing, percentage depletion allowances, price setting, discriminatory freight rates, subsidies, tax advantages, and all the other forms of direct and indirect regulation and incentives provided by the government are usually counterproductive.

Nevertheless, the government can play an active role in the energy field, but not the role of allocator and regulator that seems so attractive to the bureaucratic mind. In addition to keeping the price of energy high, the government's energy policy should probably include the following items:

- Leasing arrangements for oil and gas fields that are incentives for exploring and drilling (for example, sharing in the heavy front-end costs of offshore drilling, and sharing only in returns from gas and oil that has been actually exploited).

- Spending heavily for research and development.

- Using a negative income tax or similar policies to offset the consequences for the poor of high-priced energy. (As desirable as this solution may be, it raises a certain logical problem. With one hand the government would be raising energy prices to discourage consumption, while with the other it would be compensating the poor in a way that would allow them to consume more energy.)

- Offering incentives to improve efficiency of energy utilization. For example, tax credits might be offered for purchasing efficient automobiles, improving insulation, and replacing inefficient or polluting equipment.

- Engaging in limited antitrust activity to ensure energy competition within the national economy (recognizing that effective competition may not require a proliferation of firms).

- Deregulating transportation and other energy-intensive fields to encourage competition.

Wherever possible, efforts should be made to use market mechanisms to effect reforms. As Russell Train has recently written, "No one who has looked below the surface of the environmental issue has really believed that putting stoppers on smokestacks and out-falls has been really the most creative way to deal with pollution problems."[8] What is needed, says Train, is innovation in our production processes and the rethinking of many tried but not so well-proved industrial practices. Higher energy prices may be the best incentive for American industry to rethink many of its most basic assumptions about energy technology.

Realizing Alternative Future Opportunities through Technology
Technological determinism is one of the most uneconomical assumptions of American industry. In effect, it is widely assumed that technology like the weather is a given. Industrial engineers have led managers to believe that they must start with the machines available and then adjust all human and financial arrangements to meet the needs of the technology. It has been forgotten in Detroit, for example, that the assembly line came not from Our Maker, but from Henry Ford.

As Volvo, Saab, and others are now discovering, technology is determined by engineers and managers, not by the laws of God or nature. Simply put, there are many more options where technology is concerned than has been assumed. (This point is developed in the next section of this chapter.)

Moreover, in the energy area, there is almost complete faith border-

ing on fanaticism in the inevitability of "the grand technological solution." The orthodox vision is of a dramatic technological solution,
like some deus ex machina, descending and saving the day for modern man. Nuclear fusion, in-situ coal liquefaction, hydrogen fuel
from electrolysis, ocean thermal gradients, and solar power (either
from collectors in orbit or from collectors paving the desert) are often
advanced as attractive long-range solutions to the world's energy
problems. The grander the technology, in fact, the more attractive it
seems. After all, the bigger it is and the further off its development,
the more it will cost—which means a bigger share of a bigger pie for
everybody involved. Indeed, fusion should keep thousands of physi-
cists and engineers occupied for at least another half century—solving
the problem, at least, of unemployment among the highly skilled.

But there are several problems inherent in the big technology solution to energy problems:

- It is extremely costly, and thus requires government financing and
  consequent bureaucratic controls.

- It is difficult to estimate the effects on the environment, climate, or
  atmosphere, but by definition these are likely to be greater than with
  smaller technologies.

- Its development cannot be guaranteed—some technolgoical breakthroughs (such as antigravity) are always "just ten years away."

- Its time lag between laboratory demonstration and wide-scale commercial implementation is lengthy. For example, fission was demonstrated in 1942 but the first commercial reactor was not working until 1967. Even now, only 5 percent of U.S. electrical needs are met
  by fission. Indeed, because of environmental issues these time lags
  appear to be growing.

- Development of grand options dries up intellectual and financial capital that could be better applied to dozens of more promising less-
  expensive options.

The Delphi panel was not sanguine about grand solutions to America's energy problems. They forecast that hydrogen auto fuels and nuclear fusion will not be available for at least fifty years. They are likewise skeptical about electricity generated by centralized solar power plants; only 1 percent of U.S. electricity is forecasted to be produced in this fashion by 1995.

Nevertheless, mankind must clearly evolve from primitive energy hunters and gatherers to sophisticated energy farmers. This transformation will entail moving beyond reliance on the relatively haphazard process of discovering fossil fuels, to the scientific processes of cultivating and harvesting renewable energy derived from tides, wind, hydro, solar, chemical, and mechanical sources. This change might well include nuclear fusion someday, but possibly not soon enough to meet the inevitable running down of petroleum and natural gas resources. One thing the change implies is a long-term trend away from the centralization of energy supplies towards many decentralized, independent, alternative sources. This promises not only a more broadly based energy system (hence one less vulnerable to the vicissitudes of resource availability), but also a less bureaucratically controlled system.

The Delphi panel foresees an energy future in which oil, gas, coal, nuclear, and geothermal sources will all have a place for many generations, and these sources will be gradually augmented by solar and other currently uneconomical technologies. To ensure that these long-term changes will not lead to sudden dislocations will require the immediate initiation of some rather mundane steps: (1) conversion to a more electric economy; (2) the development of superbatteries (portable, high-energy-density, high-power-density storage devices), and (3) the gradual phasing-in of methanol as an auxiliary auto fuel.

The Advantages of Electricity   The most pressing energy problem is to reduce the consumption of petroleum and gas without creating

severe economic hardships.[9] Of the many alternatives that have been
discussed for achieving this reduction, one has received too little
attention in light of its many merits. This option is to increase the
use of more plentiful fuels by converting them to electricity. Several
major difficulties would have to be overcome to make this approach
effective, including the expensive changeover to technologies that
can utilize electricity. Still a gradual shift to an electric economy has
many distinct advantages.

First, electricity is a suitable form of energy for use with today's
plentiful coal and nuclear fuels and with most of tomorrow's pros-
pective energy sources (such as advanced nuclear, geothermal, and
solar forms). It is also a good form for converting solid waste to useful energy. Hence it is not a dead-ended medium, but one with a
flexible future. Moreover, electricity is highly versatile; it can be used
for almost every application currently satisfied by petroleum and gas,
except when these materials are used in lubrication and as feedstock
in the petrochemical industry. Finally, it is pollution-free at the use
end. This attribute, which concentrates the pollution at the genera-
tors, permits antipollution efforts to be more focused and hence
probably more effective.

Increased use of electricity poses some major associated problems:
(1) it is highly capital-intensive; (2) its use is cyclic and thus requires
a capacity that is more than double average consumption; (3) a long
time is needed to bring additional capacity into service; (4) although
it concentrates its pollution at generating stations, these stations are
major polluters (and when they are nuclear-fueled, they present
safety hazards as well as the major issue of how to dispose of radioactive wastes); and (5) the use of electricity for personal transportation appears unattractive relative to petroleum in the short run.

On the other hand, with sufficient time and capital, electricity can
easily be substituted for most industrial uses and for mass transportation. Although it is presently limited in personal transportation
vehicles by the relatively poor performance of current batteries, an
improved battery would make electric automobiles ideal replace-

ments for cars powered by internal combustion engines.

Widespread use of electric automobiles would mitigate the capital problem associated with electric power stations by reducing the cyclic use pattern of electricity; it would raise the load factor considerably. This increase would occur because electric vehicles would typically be used in the daytime and be recharged (and hence consume electricity) at night. An increased load factor would mean that less capacity would satisfy more demand; hence there would be less capital cost per unit consumed. From this perspective, increased efforts to replace petroleum- and gas-consuming devices by electrical devices is an attractive option in both the near and the longer terms.

What must still be resolved is the near-term effect that a massive switch to electricity would have on our petroleum consumption. Studies of electric automobiles have been underway for many years. These studies have failed to identify an attractive vehicle. However, they have used as their standard the performance of the internal combustion engine. If the design criteria were to develop the best transportation vehicle for use as the second (or third) car in the typical U.S. family (in an environment where petroleum is simply not available), the results might be vastly different. For example, using the present electric car, it has been shown that a 20 mph vehicle with a 50+ mile range can be developed.

Major advances have been made in electric vehicle technology in the past several years, and many light trucks and vans for urban and local delivery service may be electric-powered within the next decade. Other transportation areas that offer opportunities for electric substitution include freight and passenger trains. Similarly, it has been decades since an electrically powered trolley-bus was designed for use in American cities. Such cars, buses, trucks, and trains would offer many advantages if petroleum prices continue to rise as we envisage.

Turning to the residential sector, a comparison of gas space heating and electric heat pump environmental conditioning reveals other potential advantages of innovative uses of electricity. At present, a great fraction of residential gas and oil consumption is used in space heating while the rest is used in water heating, cooking, air conditioning, clothes drying, and other minor uses. With the application of the heat pump, space heating by electricity would offer a major savings in primary fuel use. The heat pump puts out more usable heat than it takes in as input energy. The heat energy source is the outside environment rather than fuel combustion. It is simply an air conditioning system operating in reverse. The heat pump is actually less costly than a gas furnace with air conditioning today, and will soon be less costly than a gas furnace alone as fuel prices rise in the next year or two. The commercial sector closely parallels the energy use patterns of the residential sector and therefore provides similar opportunities for electric substitution. (The heat pump is a good idea even when not generated electrically. The pump of course can be powered by any energy source.)

In the industrial sector, process steam is the largest end use of energy. In this case, the most difficult problem is the logistics of getting steam to the user. In the future, large industrial complexes could be built in clusters around steam-generating facilities.[10] In this configuration, requirements for process steam can be met by electric boilers or by waste heat from other energy conversion processes.

In summary, we are facing a period in which reducing consumption of imported petroleum and natural gas will receive the highest national priority. Domestic supplies of these fuels are declining, and new reserves have been slow in coming into the inventory. If we were to reduce consumption by fiat by rationing gasoline, we would face major economic dislocations. Hence we must gradually convert our home, industrial, and transportation energy systems to the use of more plentiful fuels. The most flexible and least disruptive way of achieving this is a gradual transition to an electric economy.

The electrical use patterns thus created would ease the capital burden on the electric utilities and would probably decrease the cost of electrical energy. Pollution and radioactive waste disposal would still be problems. But on balance, pollution would be reduced and concentrated at the generating stations. The remaining problems of waste disposal, safety, and improved batteries require further research.

The Effects of Superbatteries   One of the most remarkable forecasts made by the Delphi panel was the 50 percent probability of development of superbatteries in the next fifteen years, and 90 percent probability within twenty years.[11]

The battery may well be to the postindustrial era what the stirrup was to feudalism. Should a breakthrough in portable electrical energy storage devices occur, it would revolutionize the energy and transportation situation in America. Such a development would initially be used in electrically propelled cars, buses, and trucks. This would permit a greater shift in basic fuels from petroleum and gas to coal and nuclear. It would also change the cost trade-off associated with solar energy systems because the batteries would permit decentralized solar energy to be used and stored so that they not only provided light and heat during the night hours, but also provided energy for personal transportation vehicles.

Roof space for solar collectors would become a valuable commodity as energy provision decentralized and became an individually collected commodity. Windmills, currently inefficient largely because of a problem of storing the energy they generate, would also become a more attractive energy source. Electric utilities would become more efficient because they would be able to run their plants at maximum capacity, storing energy for use during peak periods. Inefficient electrical generation plants would be quickly phased out because the nation would have more capacity than needed.

The area of greatest growth in energy capacity would be in individual homes and commercial and industrial buildings. Utility-produced electricity would be used only to supplement energy needs that could not be met by individual systems.

This technology would also find immediate application in underdeveloped countries because it would free them from the continuous need to import petroleum. The price of petroleum would drop on the world market and the concern over its depletion would dwindle considerably. Petroleum would be used in very few applications, primarily in the petrochemical areas and for such specialized purposes as aircraft fuel.

The environmental impact of such a breakthrough would be immense. Most air pollution problems would disappear. However, the problems of transportation and traffic congestion would remain. Without the need to conserve energy, mass transportation systems may be even more difficult to implement.

The industrial activity that would be promoted by the demand for energy storage devices, solar collectors, and new vehicles would be extremely large. Many industries would also be phased out of production, leading to a major period of industrial transition.

The battery seems like such an obvious response to the problems of energy availability—then why has it received so little attention relative to other potential energy sources? Obviously, the superbattery is not, in itself, a full solution to the problems outlined above. To fully realize the potential of the battery, an efficient transducer is needed to convert sunlight into electricity. This breakthrough may be as difficult to achieve as the battery itself. Moreover, the battery is quite threatening to many large industries in the United States, most notably coal, petroleum, and autos. Still, some automakers have apparently spent research money to develop a better battery and battery-operated cars. However, because they use the performance criteria of the internal combusion engine car (speed and acceleration) in their battery vehicle designs, they find that electric cars using current lead acid batteries have a limited range (48 to 58 miles).[12]

Probably more of a constraint is that there is no battery lobby in the scientific establishment. At the National Science Foundation and the Energy Research and Development Administration big science is represented by nuclear interest groups, coal interest groups, and solar interest groups, but there just does not appear to be enough poten-

tial for big money to attract universities and private laboratories to
the relatively mundane task of developing a better battery. "Leave it
to the Japanese. There is no Nobel prize to be won in batteries," the
scientific community seems to be saying. (Indeed it appears that
Toyota has recently produced a prototype electric car with a driving
range of from 112 to 125 miles.)[13] Sadly, in the short run at least,
the scientific incentive in America seems to be working against the
development of the battery: No big research money + no moon-shot-
scale publicity + no glamour = no battery.

The Gradual Substitution of Methanol   Even without a superbattery,
some things can be done to reduce reliance on petroleum.[14] In 1975,
consumers in industrialized nations started paying a price for gasoline
at service station pumps that exceeds the costs of an equivalent
amount of energy from a nuclear reactor.[15] This little-noticed mile-
stone presages that date within the next three decades when synthetic
nonfossil fuels become cheaper than gasoline. In a paper commissioned for this study, George Hoffman has shown how synthetic
fuels will gradually come to be economical vis-à-vis fossil fuels (Exhibit 21). His econometric model shows that there will be no major
dislocations as one form of automotive fuel gradually becomes more
economical than its predecessor (the progression in his model is from
petroleum, to shale oil, to kerogen, to coal liquefaction, and ultimately to hydrogen). The price of synthetic fuel will not reach parity
with fossil fuels until the year 2025, however. Importantly, Hoffman's study indicates that it is not too early to start conceiving,
planning, and designing the nonfossil fuel industry of the next century because it will soon become economical to start using methanol
as an additive in gasoline (Exhibit 22). Hoffman has also undertaken
a cost-benefit analysis of the relative merits of methanol, cryomethane, methane, and hydrogen; he has concluded that either methanol
or cryomethane are the auto fuels of the future (Exhibits 23 and 24).
    What is significant about Hoffman's findings is that methanol, like
the superbattery, is receiving relatively little attention from industry

Exhibit 21
Probable Escalation of Automotive and Aircraft Fuel Prices

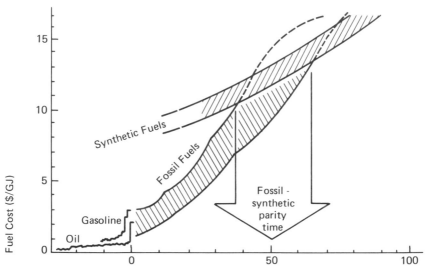

Time (years hence)

Cost of automotive and aircraft fuels in the United States will escalate and will exceed cost to synthesize nonfossil fuels in less than half a century. The band-width for fossil fuels indicates the breadth of the variety and range in those automotive energy demand and supply scenarios that were formulated in the University of Southern California econometric model. Curves are cusped at those future times when gasoline production from petroleum becomes augmented by shale oil extraction in ten or fifteen years, and by coal liquefaction into crude oil or methanol, perhaps another decade or two later. The model's scenarios included considerations of the possible penetration of battery-operated automobiles into a one-fifth or less share of the urban vehicle market.

The cost of fuels is in terms of the present value (1975 dollars) of a billion joules, GJ, of combustion energy fuel equivalent, that is, in the units of $/GJ. The heat given off by burning petroleum or released thermal energy is about 6 GJ per barrel. A good historical base point for U.S. fuel costs is 1972, when oil was around 1 $/GJ and gasoline about 1.5 times as much. By the midpoint of the 1970s these costs had escalated to 2 and 3 $/GJ.

Source: Hoffman, "The U.S. Fuel Industry in the 21st Century"

Exhibit 22
Probable Future Market Share of Synthetic Fuels

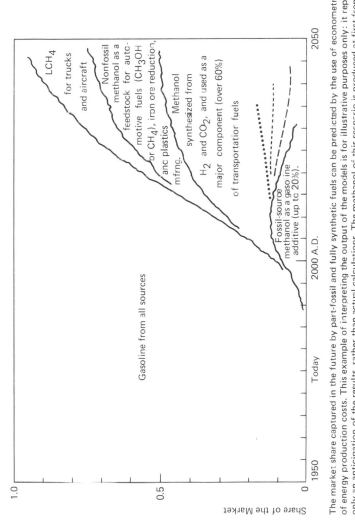

The market share captured in the future by part-fossil and fully synthetic fuels can be predicted by the use of econometric models of energy production costs. This example of interpreting the output of the models is for illustrative purposes only: it represents only an anticipation of the results, rather than actual calculations. The methanol of this scenario is produced at first from coal or from wastes and refuse, and later in the twenty-first century would be synthesized from hydrogen and carbon dioxide scavenged from air or from carbonates.

Source: Hoffman, "The U.S. Fuel Industry in the 21st Century"

Exhibit 23
Adjusting Autos to Utilize Synthetic Fuels

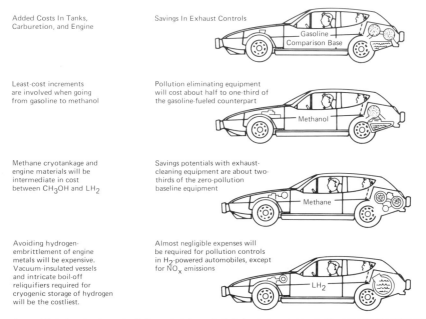

Added Costs In Tanks,
Carburetion, and Engine

Savings In Exhaust Controls

Least-cost increments
are involved when going
from gasoline to methanol

Pollution eliminating equipment
will cost about half to one-third of
the gasoline-fueled counterpart

Methane cryotankage and
engine materials will be
intermediate in cost
between CH_3OH and LH_2

Savings potentials with exhaust-
cleaning equipment are about two-
thirds of the zero-pollution
baseline equipment

Avoiding hydrogen-
embrittlement of engine
metals will be expensive.
Vacuum-insulated vessels
and intricate boil-off
reliquifiers required for
cryogenic storage of hydrogen
will be the costliest.

Almost negligible expenses will
be required for pollution controls
in H_2-powered automobiles, except
for NO_x emissions

Automobile tank, carburetor, and pollution controls for synthetic-fuel engines are compared with a conventional gasoline-powered
automobile equipped with hypothetical exhaust controls of the 1980s. The sources of potential cost or savings differences are
predicted for each type of vehicle.

Source: Hoffman, "The U.S. Fuel Industry in the 21st Century"

Exhibit 24
Costs and Benefits of Synthetic Fuels

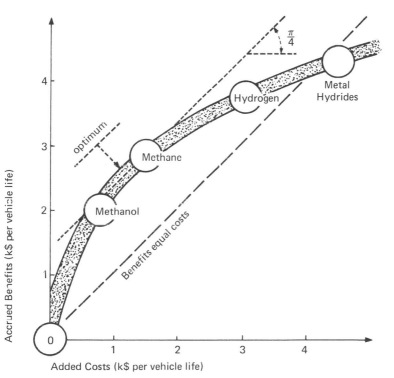

Benefit-cost plots of distant-future automotive vehicles consuming synthetic fuels point to methane and methanol as the most economic energy stores for passenger cars. The automobile used for comparing system life costs was a hypothetical zero-pollution gasoline-fueled compact passenger car residing at the origin of the benefit-cost curve. This baseline car was assumed to be designed for total elimination of contaminants from the tail pipe at the expense of filling the trunk space with pollution removal equipment and scrubbing tanks, through which the exhaust is bubbled so as to absorb or detoxify all NO_x, RCH, and CO. This exhaust control equipment was priced at $1,000 (current dollars), for acquisition and installation, plus $150 per year to maintain, service, and repair. All automotive fuel systems were assumed to use energy at the rate of 400 GJ per year during their thirteen-year life spanning that transition time, in the midst of the twenty-first century, when gasoline, methanol, methane, and hydrogen are still closely priced at 10 to 13 $/GJ. The added costs (relative to the gasoline baseline) come mainly from increasingly expensive materials and volume or mass requirements in the tanks or in the cryogenic storage vessels with reliquifiers. The added benefits are the incremental costs avoided in adopting the fuel in question. These benefit increases (or savings) are achieved in methanol-, methane-, or hydrogen-fueled autos by the decreasing cost of pollution controls and the lifetime fuel cost savings. In the equipment benefits columns, it was assumed that hydrogen was close to the almost ideal nonpolluting fuel, requiring less than $50 of capital for exhaust controls and another $50 per year for the operation of the equipment. The excess of benefits over costs for automobiles (but not for trucks or buses) is highest at the optimum between methanol and methane, where the benefit-cost curve has a slope of unity.

Source: Hoffman, "The U.S. Fuel Industry in the 21st Century"

and government.[16] Moreover, increased methanol production—when made from animal waste and garbage—like the battery, can be achieved in relatively less capital-intensive modes, in more decentralized plants, and would help to break the world's reliance on petroleum. Methanol is not as economically or socially promising as the battery, but it is ironic that the U.S. oil industry is making heavy investments in coal and shale while ignoring a potentially more acceptable source of fuel.[17] Moreover, one lesson is clear from a review of energy technologies: it is unwise to place all of one's future hopes on just one or two alternatives.

Choosing the Right Technologies: Or No Technology at All
The rising price of energy by itself will force substitution and change in the American economy. Still, choices will have to be made. Higher prices do not eliminate the need to plan—rather, they heighten the requirement to understand the long-term consequences of the options open to decision makers. For example, higher energy prices open up five aggregate alternatives:

1. Substituting energy for energy—an abundant resource like coal for a scarce one like natural gas.

2. Substituting capital for energy—adopting a new, more energy-efficient technology.

3. Substituting a product for energy—making a dress out of cotton rather than nylon, or making liquid detergents rather than powdered detergents.

4. Substituting processes for energy—installing windows that open in office buildings.

5. Substituting labor for energy—assembling a radio by hand instead of mechanically.

Which of these substitutions to make will depend on the industry in question and on the analysis of the second- and third-order conse-

quences of the alternatives. Businessmen, economists, and engineers
tend to favor the first two options because these are consistent with
the traditional concepts of economic efficiency. However, changes in
values, new environmental concerns, and notions of corporate social
responsibility will force future-oriented executives to weigh also the
costs and benefits of the latter three forms of substitutions.

Especially important in such deliberations will be choosing technologies appropriate to the future. In the past, the appropriate type
and scale of technology could be determined through the optimiza-
tion of what economists call "production functions," which are
basically equations used to find the best mix of labor, capital, and
natural resources to produce a good. It is unlikely that industrialists
will be able to rely only on this quantitative method of achieving
profit maximization in the future. "The one best way," "optimiza-
tion," "maximization," and "industrial efficiency" are, as Daniel Bell
reminds us, not the only concepts that will impinge themselves on
the decision-making process in industry in the late twentieth century.
Already, industrial organizations are finding that society will not permit them to pursue a single goal (profit maximization). Indeed, as executives of most of the leading firms in America are beginning to recognize, businesses are becoming social institutions with many consti-
tuencies and many goals. As we see today, businesses are not only
under pressure from stockholders to use capital efficiently to increase
productivity and profits, there are new pressures, too: from conserva-
tionists to use processes that are environmentally sound, from the
government to use energy efficiently, from consumers to produce
safe and durable goods, from unions and society to create jobs, and
from workers to provide satisfying jobs.

The traditional task of managers of choosing the right technologies
and the right production mix is therefore more important than ever,
but the factors influencing their decisions are concomitantly more
complex and the consequences of their options less clear. A new calculus will be needed for effectively choosing technologies in the
future. This calculus—if it can be called that—must incorporate the

new qualitative concerns of the society along with the traditional
quantitative concerns of management for industrial efficiency.

How would this calculus be applied? There is no reason to believe
that there will be any magic formula—technologies and processes will
differ from industry to industry and from plant to plant. Nor is there
any reason to predict a sudden and massive abandoning of current
plants and machines. More likely, the shift will be gradual as new
plants and equipment are introduced to replace obsolete capital
goods. Within these broad parameters, it will probably be necessary
for future executives to choose processes that move toward the ends
of the technological continuum illustrated in Exhibit 25 and away
from the middle-range technologies that were developed in the latter
part of the industrial era.[18]

It is clear that middle-level technologies are suited for industrial
eras characterized by cheap energy, surplus capital, high consumer
demand for mass-produced goods, little environmental concern, and
a poorly educated work force. Because the future appears antithetical
to all these characteristics, it seems likely that industry will move
either to the high productivity of high technology or to the high quality of low technology.

In the auto industry, for example, growing pressures for energy and
capital efficiency, productivity, and worker satisfaction would probably lead managers over the next twenty years to produce cars using
either fully automated processes (an assembly line without semiskilled production workers) or by teams of highly skilled manual
workers. Which way the industry or company will go will depend on
the price of its product, union pressures, and dozens of other factors
too numerous to list here. What is important is that it is improbable
that the industry will be able to stay in the middle of the continuum.
Moreover, moving either way from the center will require the invention of new technologies.

Low-technology solutions need not entail a return to backbreaking
labor. For example, Volvo has shown that new low technologies can
be highly productive and laborsaving, and require as much engineering genius as high technologies. In its plant at Kalmar, Sweden, Volvo

Exhibit 25
The Technological Continuum

	Low Technology	Middle Technology	High Technology
	← ———————————————— Trend ———————————————— →
1. Energy efficiency	Very high	Low	Medium
2. Capital use efficiency	High	Medium	Very high
3. Productivity	Medium/Low	Medium	Very high
4. Quality of goods	High	Low	High
5. Environmental soundness	High	Low	Medium
6. Worker satisfaction	Very high	Low	High
7. Labor intensity	Very high	Medium/Low	Medium/High

has replaced the assembly line with 250 individual car carriers—18-foot long platforms that deliver cars to 25 different assembly teams. Not only is the monotony of the assembly line avoided, the painful necessity of working in the uncomfortable overhead position typical of assembly lines has been replaced by the ability of the car carriers to be tipped on their side, thus allowing the worker to perform his tasks at a normal eye-level position. What is being discovered around the world is that there is *choice* where technology is concerned. A Mead company paper mill in the South has recently designed its technology to meet human needs instead of arranging human organization to meet the needs of technology. The entrepreneurial challenge is to find technologies that are environmentally sound, energy-efficient, and satisfying for workers.

What would happen to productivity if substitutes were made to the low rather than the high end of the continuum? E. F. Schumacher argues that the gross productivity of society can actually be increased by applying the appropriate technologies:

As I have shown, directly productive time in our society has already been reduced to about 3½ percent of "total social time" [all the collective time of adults, including sleeping, eating, watching television, and doing jobs that are not directly productive] , and the whole drift of modern technological development is to reduce it further, asymptotically, to zero. Imagine we set ourselves a goal in the opposite direction—to increase it sixfold, to about twenty percent, so that twenty percent of the total social time would be used for actually producing things, employing hands and brains and, naturally, excellent tools. . . . At one-sixth of present-day productivity, we should be producing as much as at present. There would be six times as much time for any piece of work we choose to undertake—enough to make a really good job of it, to enjoy oneself, to produce real quality, even to make things beautiful.[19]

The technological continuum illustrates not only the alternatives for a given industry but also the probable general drift of the American economy as a whole. What is important to understand about the aggregate effects of a shift from middle technologies is

- The shifts will be gradual.

- The shifts will go both ways—not just to the high or just to the low end. The Schumacher view that only small is beautiful is inappropriate in our advanced economy. The high productivity of high technology actually helps to support more workers in services and low technology jobs.

- We do not know which industries will go which way at this time.

- The shifts will be voluntary responses to market and social pressures.

- Shifts to low technology do not necessarily entail abandoning modern technology or high productivity.

Basically, the shifts forecasted have four antecedents in the contemporary economy. First, the United States is already moving toward a services economy and beginning to rely on foreign nations to provide many mass-produced and some energy-intensive goods. These shifts are likely to continue for as long as there is a less-developed world and for as long as some underdeveloped countries have ready access to cheap natural gas and oil. Second, American industries are beginning to adopt the so-called sociotechnical philosophy that technologies can be designed to meet social needs. Third, there is some rekindled interest in the production of goods by craftsmen.

Fourth, some mass-produced goods that contribute only to waste or planned obsolescence are being abandoned (beverage cans). None of these incipient trends constitutes a revolution. But it is not a revolution that is being forecast. Rather, it would seem that higher energy costs, when combined with the larger package of new social and economic demands, will encourage substitutions of products or processes or labor for energy.

Effects of Substitutions of Products   The basic assumption underlying all discussions of substitutions in this report is that these will and must be only marginal substitutions designed to accomplish change without major dislocations. It is commonly assumed that something like 8 percent of the capital stock in America is replaced in a typical year; it may be possible to achieve meaningful changes within this normal increment and thus avoid abrupt economic and social dislocations.

Immediately, when one speaks of substitutions among the goods provided and consumed in America, two bogey issues are raised:

- Products will be arbitrarily banned by the government.

- True laborsaving devices such as clothes washers will be replaced by outmoded and dehumanizing technologies such as hand wringers and washboards.

First of all, substitutions must be economical. It is assumed that the higher price of energy will make the substitutions into sound economic decisions by business and consumers. Second, the substitutions will only occur where the consumer sees benefit: for example, iceboxes would not be competitive with refrigerators even if the cost of energy were quintupled. Rather, as Amana has demonstrated, an advanced, insulated refrigerator that saves about $50 a year in electric costs can be sold for about $100 more than a conventional model.

Product substitutions are most likely to occur where there is obvious waste. For example, laundry detergents are first made as liquids and are then converted in a second energy-consuming process to

powder—only to be inevitably converted back to liquid detergents in
washing machines. One would expect the higher prices of energy to
make liquid detergents more attractive. The problem in the short run
is that there are very few producers of detergents, and each one
knows that the others will not start pricing liquid detergents lower
than powdered detergents because each has a huge marketing investment in powdered products. This is probably a strategy that will only
work in the short run, however. In the long run, one or the other of
the following is likely to occur:

- First consumer journals and then the popular press will realize that
  liquids are potentially cheaper than powders. In response to high
  potential demand, one of the oligopolists will drop his prices for
  liquids.

- The price of powdered detergents will go so high that consumers will
  start substituting soap, thus forcing the detergent manufacturers to
  retaliate with their least-expensive product—liquids.

- The Fair Trade Commission or the Justice Department will bring
  price-fixing charges against the detergent manufacturers.

    One way or another, the substitutions will be made. Clearly, the
more competitive the market the more efficient and less bureaucratic
the substitutions will be. Other likely product substitutions include
paper for plastics in packaging; cotton, linen, wool, glass, fiber and
hemp for rayon, nylon, and polyesters; natural oil and resins for a
large share of the plastics in paint and films; natural fertilizers for
some petrochemical fertilizers (one is already noticing a bucolic odor
on the streets of suburbia as chemical lawn food has soared upward
to $12 for a 25 lb bag); and natural rubber for synthetic rubber.
    None of these changes will be abrupt or complete, but such substi-
tutions will occur. Most important, most of these substitutions need
not entail any great reduction in the quality of life. For example, energy-saving fluorescent lamps and heat pumps are not poor cousin
substitutes for incandescent lamps and old-fashioned forced-air gas

furnaces. It can even be argued that higher energy prices might herald
a Quality Economy, in which many mass-produced, short-lived goods
will be replaced by durable, repairable high-quality goods. Under such
a transformation, America would become more like it was before
World War II or like Europe is today. America would still be a consumer society, but purchases would be made more carefully and the
quality of a good would be a more important consideration than its
low initial price. Such a shift does not necessarily presage either inflation or unemployment. If a quality good costs three times as much
as a mass-produced good, it might also be expected to last three times
as long, use three times less energy and natural resources, use three
times the labor, and give its consumers three times the pleasure because it does not break or wear out as soon as they get it home from
the store. This shift would be noticed first in autos, furniture, wearing apparel, toys, appliances, and the other so-called durables of the
age of planned obsolescence.

Effects of Process Substitution   The effects of a shift to a Quality
Economy would probably be most spectacular in architecture. Ralph
Knowles of the USC Architectural School notes that because of en-
ergy shortages there will be

a changed growth mode in the future, rather than a cessation of
growth. What some would term recycling, I call transformation.
Whichever term is used, the process involves rebuilding and reorgan-
izing the existing city, rather than continuing its expansion.[20]

Knowles has used computers to help design buildings that mitigate
the effects of daily and yearly thermal variations. Combating the
anachronistic "build-cheap, maintain-expensive" mentality of builders, it is now possible to design buildings that use nature to accomplish much of the heating and cooling that has been done by expensive air conditioners and furnaces—costs not usually borne by build-

ers or developers but by future owners and occupants. Ironically, Knowles's computer shows that the design of the future will be quite close to that of the Indian pueblos of the Southwest. One interesting characteristic of such buildings will be that each of the three, four, five, or twenty-five sides (or faces) of the structure will be different from the others to maximize the positive effects of insolation.

The technology for such changes is available. But here is another case where the cultural paradigms of the industrial era are currently inhibiting the fullest use of energy-efficient technology. Apparently, builders and their clients are not ready to accept the new shape of energy-efficient architecture because it violates their concept of what a building should look like. The inheritance of nineteenth-century formalism in design and uniformity for production purposes limits the spread of architectural innovation.

Again, the free market with its promise of greater choice is inhibited by cultural constraints and restrictive economic practices. Most singularly, change is thwarted by the misconception that energy-saving design ipso facto translates into a reduced quality of life. "To the contrary," Knowles writes, "it may well be that energy-conserving urban design will provide greater diversity and greater choice than we enjoy at present."[21]

One measure of this potential for greater diversity is the pleasant trend toward renovating old buildings in response to the capital and energy crunches. According to a survey in *Buildings* in 1975, nearly 15,000 old office buildings are being modernized at a cost of $12 billion, up 38 percent from a 1971 survey.[22] With the costs of energy-intensive bricks, steel, and aluminum climbing, it is now becoming cheaper to keep old buildings with natural air conditioners (windows that open) and humanistic design (high ceilings, broad corridors, bathrooms with marble fixtures).

Changes in architecture and industrial processes are likely to come about when decision makers and investors start to become more sensitive to the hidden costs of their current practices and to the potential benefits inherent in alternatives. For example, although watching

television is a practice that has been rated relatively low in terms of
energy consumption, the Associated Press reports that it requires 400
gallons of water to provide the steam (and then to cool the steam in
an electric power plant) for a night's TV viewing in a single household.[23] Such cases clearly call for an understanding of alternative
and secondary uses of the steam produced. In this regard, better insulation, recuperation, regeneration, and other housekeeping activities offer potential for industrial savings as Dow Chemical has recently demonstrated.[24]

Some process changes do not even require new capital. A change in
government regulations to encourage the movement of scrap metals
by train would lead to enormous energy savings through recycling,
for example. And "recycled aluminum requires only 5 percent as
much energy to process as primary aluminum."[25] In the past, energy
has contributed only about 5 percent to value added in industry.
Consequently, there was no incentive to recycle or make other process substitutions. Now, with the cost of energy rising faster than the
other factors of production, greater recycling is likely. Realistically,
however, one cannot expect too much from recycling in the short
run. America is currently recycling less than at any time in its history, and the Delphi panel feels it will take some time to reverse the
trend. The panel estimates that about 10 percent of total energy use
in the United States could be saved through recycling. They estimate
that only about 2 percent is saved in this way today, and that the
savings will climb slowly to 5 percent in 1985 and 6 percent in 1995.

Recycling alone offers rather unspectacular savings, but *in addition
to* substitutions with other new industrial technologies and processes
the potential savings are tremendous. The activities of consumers
also only offer small savings, but in the aggregate these too loom
large. Such consumer process substitutions as cold water washing, re-
moving pilot lights on ovens, turning down thermostats, and car
pooling altogether could save the equivalent of 2 million barrels of
oil a day, according to the Federal Energy Administration.

Higher energy prices will lead to changes in the activities of con-

sumers. During the energy crisis, Ted Bartell of UCLA measured its
effects on the attitudes and life-styles of Los Angeles residents.[26] He
found that even though many people suspected they were being manipulated by the oil companies and the then president, almost all at-
temped to conserve energy (see Exhibit 26), and few people felt that
these changes in behavior had more than a minimal effect on their
lifestyles. People expressed the greatest concern about potential difficulties in getting to work.

Although getting to work presents the greatest obstacles to changing the energy-consuming behavior of the citizenry, George Gallup
reports that fully two-thirds of Americans feel they could solve this
problem even without a car.[27]

In architecture, industry, commerce, and transportation, there is
thus clearly more room for substitution without hardship than the
nation's industrial and political leaders have been willing to admit.
For example, according to Glenn Seaborg, Porsche recently introduced a car at an auto show in Germany that has a lifespan of
twenty years or 200,000 miles—but it reportedly withdrew the car
from display with assurances to its competitors in the auto industry

Exhibit 26
Measures Taken to Reduce Energy Consumption

Always tried to turn off lights when not needed	93%
Reduced heating or turned down thermostats	80%
Drove less to places of recreation	69%
Not taken Sunday drives or other drives for pleasure	67%
Visited friends or relatives less often	61%
Shopped less often or closer to home	58%
Replaced light bulbs with smaller bulbs	52%
Used appliances like washers and toasters less	48%
Not taken a vacation trip	38%
Watched television less	37%
Changed way of travel to work or school	18%

Source: Bartell, "The Effects of the Energy Crisis on Attitudes and Lifestyles of Los
Angeles Citizens"

that it had no intention of marketing it.[28] Moreover, many of the
postwar substitutions that occurred in search of reliability and durability now have come themselves to be obsolete: for example, nylon
stockings are no longer everlasting.

The first task is to face the fact that substitutions in goods and
processes are now necessary as a result of higher energy prices. The
second task is to accept the challenge of Buckminster Fuller—we
need not accept less as a consequence of resource limitations if we
apply our imaginations to "getting more from less."

Effects of Substitution of Labor   A great deal of literature considers
the capital-labor relationship in production. Basically, these studies
suggest that capital and labor are substitutes (as measured, for example, by the elasticity of substitution). However, in most of these
studies energy does not formally appear as an input into the production process. Until recently, the price of energy relative to capital and
labor was very low—so low in fact that most economic researchers
appear to have treated it essentially as a free good. The result is that
to date measures of energy-capital or energy-labor substitutions are
very sparse. Consequently, precise statements about the nature of the
several relationships involved in capital-labor-energy productivity are
extremely difficult to make. Fortunately, though, some recent work
is beginning to come to light. Brendt and Wood have found that capital and energy appear to be complements.[29] Their estimate of the
elasticity of substitution suggests that, other things being held constant, a 1 percent increase in relative energy prices would reduce the
demand for capital goods by between 0.14 and 0.16 percent. This result, coupled with the substitution relationship between capital and
labor, suggests that labor and energy must be substitutes. In short,
economists would expect an increase in relative energy prices to cause
a substitution of labor for capital goods.

The United States may already be witnessing some marginal and
temporary substitution of labor for capital as a result of rising energy
prices. Why would the increased cost of energy lead to a substitution

of labor for capital? In the past, industry could always assume that energy would be abundant and cheap. Because it takes energy to produce and to drive machines and because energy was viewed as almost a free good, the cost of capital goods was relatively cheap compared to the continually soaring costs of labor. Therefore cheap energy increased the attractiveness of capital over labor. (Capital and energy were also made more competitive with labor through such government policies as capital depreciation and oil and gas depletion tax write-offs.)

Today the price of energy is starting to reflect its real costs (see Chapter 2); this in turn is driving up the initial and lifetime costs of machines. Some data presented earlier are instructive on this point. Between 1920 and 1960, the amount of energy needed to produce each dollar of GNP fell gradually and irregularly. But beginning in the late 1960s, this trend started to reach a plateau, creeping upward even before the oil embargo caused its reversal in 1974. Also, a trace of evidence from the Delphi study now shows that the ratio of wages to the cost of energy (and to the cost of machinery) will be starting to decrease for the first time since economists began to make accurate estimates of these indicators. Agriculture and industry yield some recent evidence of at least some marginal substitution of labor for capital. (It is possible, however, that this is merely a measure of a temporary reallocation of manpower to patch leaky gas pipes, to improve insulation, and to perform other such chores.)

This much is easy. The difficult analysis occurs when one attempts to estimate just where the substitution of labor for capital and energy will occur. The problem is that there is no such thing as energy, capital, or labor—these are merely abstractions. Economists delineate five different types of energy and thousands of different kinds of capital goods. And theoretically at least, each of the hundred million people in the U.S. labor force has distinct characteristics. How then can one disaggregate? Suppose we disaggregate capital into three types—capital used for production purposes, capital used for energy conservation (insulation), and capital that has an environmental use (pollution abatement equipment). Then for the sake of argument, assume there

exists only one type of energy and one type of labor. Even in this
simple case, the number of substitution possibilities has increased
dramatically. Observe the possibility that increased energy prices may
now cause the substitution of one type of capital for another without any fundamental changes in the basic model. An increase in the
complexities of the substitution process possible here might result in
the situation that an increase in energy prices might leave labor being
complementary with certain types of capital and substitutable for
other types. The possibilities are myriad.

The only option in this report is to use aggregate analyses. In the
future, then, if energy prices continue to rise, we are likely to see a
major reordering of the relative weights given to the factors of production. Thus, the historical trend of substituting capital and natural
resources for labor will most probably be slowed, if not reversed. In
the future, industries and nations may have to move in the direction
of better utilization of the most important, resilient, and least tapped
factor of production—humans.

Need such a reformulation result in return to toil and drudgery?
Need the quality of life be reduced? Must there be a neo-Luddite
revolution in which technology is exorcised from the body economic?

There is some reason to believe that a carefully planned, limited,
and executed policy of pursuing more labor-intensive activities could
lead in quite the opposite direction—to the Quality Economy in
which conditions of life at work and at leisure are significantly en-
hanced. And far from this change requiring a mindless destruction or
rejection of technology, it could utilize those existing and new technologies that are on the far ends of the technological spectrum.

The rising price of energy and the shift to more labor-intensive
activities as the result of market pressures are likely to have some
startling social and economic consequences. Most basically, these
shifts will challenge the common wisdom concerning economic policy, as expressed in a recent *Wall Street Journal* editorial:

A society increases its standard of living primarily by increasing the
capital input relative to the labor input. A worker can enjoy a sus-

tained increase in his standard of living only if he becomes more productive. And sustained increases in productivity come from supplying
better tools, that is, by investing more capital.

Of course, it is as close to fact as one can get to assert that the
process of economic growth *has occurred* through the substitution of
capital for labor. Historically, such growth has been at the core of
much of mankind's social and political progress and economic developments.[30]

But in the future a counterargument may run as follows. If the
further substitution of capital for labor along the lines the *Journal*
advocates leads to greater pollution, the inefficient use of energy and
other scarce resources, increased inflation, unemployment (and dis-
satisfying jobs for those lucky enough to find employment), in what
real sense will this substitution enhance the standard of living?

In the changing social values of society, many observers are beginning to see the makings of a new set of measures of progress. Of
course, these values are represented in only one among many competing cultural strains in society, and they may not come to dominate. Nor is it clear that society would be better off were they to
dominate in a pure or dogmatic form. Nevertheless, among increasing
numbers of Americans, there is an apparent shift in values from the
primacy of the *quantity* of goods (Veblen's "conspicuous consumption" or Bell's "economizing mode") to a concern with the *quality*
of life. Even among economists, measures of industrial efficiency now
find counterparts in measures of social efficiency, as those who once
spoke of "free goods" now speak of "externalities."

On all fronts, there appears to have been a fundamental shift to
concern for the human in economic activity. This is most clearly seen
in the current and widespread efforts to improve the quality of working life in Europe and America.[31] It is being argued that much of the
technology that has been associated with substitutions of capital for
labor (assembly lines) has led to the dehumanization of the activity
at which people spend most of their waking hours. With one hand,

the benefits resulting from such substitutions are fostering high expectations among the citizenry, while with the other hand taking
away much that was challenging, satisfying, and rewarding from work.
E. J. Mishan and others are now asking to what extent the material
gadgetry and gimmickry produced by timesaving machines has com-
pensated the worker for the dull, onerous, repetitive, and spirit-des-
troying tasks he must undertake to earn these.[32] Much recent research indicates that satisfaction with work is a prime determinant of
the quality of life for most people. Hence, future attempts to improve
material well-being through the substitution of capital for labor will
be greatly constrained by the necessity to make such efforts also improve the quality of work.

In the future, the policies of a Quality Economy may have three
goals:

- To reduce pollution-causing waste and inefficient use of energy and
  other raw materials.

- To create full employment in meaningful jobs.

- To produce goods and services that enhance the quality of life.

Could these goals be reached in a democratic free-market society?
The social and political technology for such an economy may already
be at hand. According to Bruce Hannon, the process might start with
a reordering of public expenditures.[33] This would not entail a greater
role for government, but rather the acceptance by government of the
above three goals as criteria for choosing among alternative purchases
of public goods. What is required is not a revolution, but a marginal
changeover in the goods and services that society chooses to produce
and to consume. In choosing whether America should invest a billion
dollars in one alternative or another, Congress would make its decision on the basis of which alternative is the most resource-efficient,
labor-intensive, and quality-of-life-enhancing. For example, for an
identical investment of $5 billion, the government could create either
423,000 new jobs with a health program or 256,000 with a highway

program.[34] Given almost this exact choice, the American government recently chose the latter. In a Quality Economy, the consequences of such investments would be known to politicians and to the public, and the investment decision could be made on the three objective criteria laid out above. According to Hannon, the opportunities for using public policy in this way are enormous. For example, America could create 30,000 new jobs by requiring that returnable bottles be used in place of throwaway cans, and 30 billion kilowatt hours of electricity could be saved in the process. Hannon has created a model of the economy that demonstrates the employment and energy consequences of using $5 billion of federal highway expenditures on alternative programs:

Program	Percentage of energy saving over highway program	Percentage of employment increase over highway program
Mass transit	61.6	3.2
Educational facilities	37.1	4.7
Law enforcement	−3.4	53.6
National health insurance	64.0	65.2
Tax relief	23.4	7.4
Water and waste facilities	41.7	1.3

Source: Roger Bezdek and Bruce Hannon, "Energy, Manpower, and the Highway Trust Fund"

Such analysis is, of course, incomplete. It leaves out such considerations as whether new highways are needed more than health insurance and what the nature of the jobs being created might be. But the figures do suggest that a Quality Economy might be able to support an advanced nation without significantly reducing the standard of living of the people. Clearly, the restoration of our air, water, and cities might constitute the basis for a many billion dollar economy.[35] The end of planned obsolescence might conserve energy and resources and create meaningful work and quality goods. A shift to higher aesthetic standards in architecture and consumer products, to goods that are more durable, and to greater emphasis on recycling could all contribute to the three goals of the Quality Economy.

Contrary to the arguments advanced by many labor leaders, machines in the aggregate are not replacing workers to any great extent. Rather, as a society, America is choosing or encouraging the production of goods and services that are highly capital-intensive. In the future, there is likely to be pressure to choose otherwise. But there will probably not be a massive turning against technology; rather, pressures will be brought to utilize technologies at the extreme ends of the technological spectrum that enhance the goals of a Quality Economy. For example, many new technologies in energy, communications, transportation, cybernetics, health, and food production clearly meet the quality criteria.

This means that a Quality Economy might be characterized by high productivity and low inflation (see the arguments presented about inflation in Chapter 3), and still have growth as a major component, although not as the primary goal. It is clearly possible and desirable to have economic growth that is not damaging to the environment and that increases the quality of work, life, and goods. For example, increases in the productivity of professionals and service workers would probably have positive consequences for the Quality Economy.

Most economists assume that an advanced economy that becomes more labor-intensive will have problems with unemployment, hardships for the poor, and social class antagonism. As proof, evidence from depressions is often adduced. But Mishan has argued that there is a difference in consequences between when a growth-predicated economy stagnates and when a Quality Economy is functioning at its normal rate.[36] The goal is not to create a stagnating economy but rather a vigorous economy in which the norm is full employment even without heavy capital investment in middle-range technologies.

The unanswered question is whether increased substitution of labor for capital is an unmitigated step backward to a lower standard of living. There is a clear danger that such an economy could stagnate and lead to a cessation of artistic, medical, scientific, and social progress. Ten years ago this problem would have been threatening. But tomorrow's high energy prices, shortages of capital, environmental problems, and changes in values may moot the issue. For example, a major manpower problem facing America in the next three decades will be underemployment—the underutilization of skills, training, education, and other human resources. About 80 percent of all recent college graduates are underemployed, and about 35 percent of all workers report that their potential is not being realized on their jobs.[37] It is possible that developing these human resources more fully is the technological challenge of the Quality Economy, just as the development of better tools and machines was the ultimate source of productivity in industrial society.

Moving the economy from the center of the technological spectrum to the two ends would thus not only create good, meaningful jobs in energy- and capital-saving industries but it might also have a positive effect on national productivity by tapping the latent and growing reserves of human resources.

It is not clear, of course, whether these substitutions of goods, processes, and labor for energy will or should occur. But it is necessary that decision makers familiarize themselves with the possible costs and benefits of the full array of options before them. However, choosing wisely among the options will require more than just familiarity with the costs and benefits of each alternative. Future-oriented decisions require imagination, innovation, incentive, and an entrepreneurial spirit. What is the likelihood that these managerial resources will be abundant in the coming decades?

Innovation and Competition: The Missing Ingredients
The entrepreneur is a futurist par excellence. He has a vision of where the world is heading—or where he thinks it should head—and he sets about making plans and using his resources to realize his vision. Somehow, this ability to visualize the future—and to remain true to that vision in the face of powerful naysayers—has been lost to a great extent in contemporary America. Americans were once the world's inventors, innovators, and entrepreneurs. Today, American business

leaders with vision are often reviled in the press as fanatics, loners, and egotists. In large corporations, the incentives are often not for risk takers, but for those who prize security. The results for American industry are disastrous. Detroit auto technology has remained relatively unchanged since the late 1940s when automatic transmissions, power brakes, and air conditioners were introduced. Since then almost all major innovations from gas-conserving engines to seat belts have been of foreign origin.[38] A standard joke was once that the Japanese could only copy American technology; today Americans copy the Japanese in many fields.

The lack of imagination is worse, if anything, in government. Congressional responses to such perennial issues as unemployment, inflation, and welfare are to rehash the policies of the New Deal. Moreover, the new problems of health and safety, consumerism, and the environment are typically addressed by imposing regulations that are complex, unwieldly, and counterproductive. For example, the remedy for industrial pollution of waterways is to set arbitrary standards for cleanliness (raising the unresolvable issues of how clean is clean and how much marginal effort should be made to clean relatively pure water). The alternative approach—the internalization of costs—is more attractive, but still leaves open such problems as determining costs and what to do about companies who are willing to pay to pollute. The typical governmental solutions to water pollution, then, do more for economists, lawyers, and bureaucrats than for clean rivers, lakes, and streams.

Although we choose not to pursue them, there are imaginative alternatives to the standard operating procedures. For example, the government could pass a law stating simply that the clean water intake for a factory must be downstream from the point where it discharges water. Such a law would be unambiguous and possibly more effective than the policies we have tried.

It is ironic that America—once known as the world's great experimentor—is today an importer of social, economic, and technological ideas from other industrialized countries.[39] In the last decade, three trends have conspired to remove the incentive to innovate from the American system:

• An increasingly heavy reliance on government to make decisions and to finance change.

• A growing lack of competition among major American industries.

• A continuing commitment to public and private managerial practices and beliefs that were appropriate for the 1950s, but are anachronistic today.

The ability to respond to the energy challenges of the long-range future hinges upon the rekindling of the nation's entrepreneurial imagination. The current environment discourages bold views of the future. There has been so much security in the status quo that there was little incentive to plan ahead for a better tomorrow. But the long-range consequence of present security is an insecure future. To a degree, success has spoiled America. The easy success of the booming 1950s and '60s led the nation to forget that the wellspring of its innovative spirit was not the government or even large multinational corporations. The historical source of entrepreneurial incentive is competition. As there has never been any other source of the spirit in the industrial sector, it is likely then that competition will be a necessary precondition for innovation in the future as well.

In the American context, competition means that decisions are made by future-oriented entrepreneurs operating in a relatively unconstrained marketplace. The effects on energy policy of a revitalization of market mechanisms would be enormous. For example, under government control the key question of future energy use has become conservation. Under a market system, the key question facing competing planners would be the efficient use of resources—all resources, not simply energy. This difference in perspective opens a wider range of options to society and eliminates much of the danger of an energy-focused policy that might well optimize the energy sub-

system, but would move the entire economic system away from opti-
mality. The central economic issue of the efficient allocation of resources is so complex that it cannot be optimally accomplished by
central planners (as the Russians have proved); it must be done by
millions of individual planners—businessmen and consumers.

Several suggestions for change have been advanced to facilitate
more efficient market responses to the issue of energy scarcity. For
example, it is generally conceded that the deregulation of the price
of natural gas would increase exploration for (and discovery of) new
sources of this valuable resource. Even in the unlikely event that new
discoveries were insignificant, deregulation would still result in a
much better allocation of existing supplies by allowing interstate
users to bid effectively against intrastate consumers (whose bid prices
are currently beyond the jurisdiction of the Federal Power Commission). Higher prices would also make various conservation efforts
more cost-effective than at present. Likewise, higher prices would encourage the development of substitute sources of energy. In fact,
there was a comparable situation involving West Virginia and Ohio
during the 1916-1922 period.[40] At that time, West Virginia produced
substantial amounts of natural gas from Appalachian fields. Much of
the gas was sold in interstate markets to Ohio and Pennsylvania.
When production in the fields peaked and began to decline, these
states bid the gas away from West Virginia users. (This was possible
because West Virginia prices were regulated by a state commission,
but prices in interstate markets were not.) West Virginia attempted
to control the export of gas, but this was held to be unconstitutional.
The only alternatives were to let the price rise or extend regulation
to interstate commerce. Ultimately, the latter course was chosen by
the federal government, leading eventually to the present depression
of natural gas prices and the resulting scarcity.

Similarly, it has been suggested that a more efficient system of surface transportation could be developed if the Interstate Commerce
Commission were stripped of its power to control the entry, exit,
and rates of the trucking industry. The immediate effect of this

would be to lower transportation costs significantly. Some carriers
would probably be forced out of business by the competition, and
railroads would largely drive truckers out of the long-haul business.
To the extent that increased use of railroads resulted, energy conservation would be increased. Cheaper transportation also has many
other advantages. For example, lower transport costs increase the
degree of competition in the economy by expanding the effective
competitive range of firms. Likewise, it frees resources that can be
put to use in more productive enterprises.

A somewhat similar situation exists in local transportation markets.
Historically, the subsidized construction of highways and freeways
had the effects of reducing population densities while simultaneously
reducing the cost of private vehicle transportation (particularly the
time costs). As a result, formerly profitable private bus and trolley
companies became insolvent and were purchased by ever-expanding
local governmental transportation agencies. To protect themselves
from competition, private transit companies and their public succes-
sors succeeded in strictly limiting the ability of cabs, jitneys, and private bus lines to compete with their monopolies.[41] Faced with public
transportation and all its disadvantages, most travelers switched to
private cars. Thus, private vehicle use was given an artificial stimulus
by the controls imposed on taxis, jitneys, and other private transit
companies. Because cabs and jitneys offer much of the flexibility
found in private automobiles, they would seem to represent likely
substitutes for private cars—but artificial limits on entry and artificially high fares still effectively eliminate cabs and jitneys from
much of this market. As fuel prices climb, deregulation of local transportation could provide substantial fuel and efficiency savings. Freed
from the artificial limits on fares, routes, and number of passengers,
cabs and jitneys would almost certainly drive buses out of some markets. But at the same time, they would lure commuters out of their
private cars by offering almost the same speed, safety, comfort, and
conveniences of the private automobile—without the substantial investment necessary to purchase and operate one. These multipassen-

ger vehicles would be utilized much more efficiently than private cars. The net effect of all this on energy consumption is not entirely clear. Buses would suffer a loss in patronage and would therefore have to reduce service (in the aggregate) from present levels. But the remaining financially viable routes would utilize fuel much more efficiently. Taxis and jitneys would consume more fuel because of the increased scope of their operations, but there would also be a decrease in the use of private vehicles in favor of the more fuel efficient cabs. The overall effect could be to increase the total demand for public transportation, which might actually increase the total amount of fuel burned (although it would be used more efficiently). It is more likely, however, that the net effects would be both less consumption of energy and more efficient use of it.

Charging for the use of freeway space is a related market-oriented proposal for increasing the efficiency of local transportation and thus using less fuel.[42] Simplified to its essentials, the proposal is directed at the problem that freeways are currently not being used in an efficient manner. Normally, these roads are designed for peak-load traffic. If the roads efficiently handle peak-load traffic, they are underutilized for the rest of the day. Frequently, peak-load traffic is also congested. The economic problem lies in the fact that when Carl Commuter chooses to drive on a freeway, he must bear certain costs—time, variable costs, and portions of the fixed cost of the vehicle—but not other costs such as the delay to all other drivers that one additional car on the freeway creates. Thus, the problem is an externality—Carl does not bear the full social costs of his activity (driving on the freeway). As a result, utilization of the freeways is inefficient—Carl might be willing to pay to get home faster during rush hour but cannot do so. Problems of fuel consumption and air pollution also result from the inefficient system of allocating freeway space. The idling and stop and go driving of rush hour traffic jams not only results in less efficient vehicle fuel consumption, but also increases the pollution-emissions level when compared to the uncongested steady flow of traffic. Another substantial source of savings in energy and other resources of a meter system would be the savings inherent in not building (or expanding) freeways to handle the peak loads. Instead, the price for road use during the peaks would be raised relative to other periods, thereby encouraging a more constant level of road usage—while at the same time providing substantial incentives to private motorists to use more people-intensive transportation. For example, if the price for commuting to downtown Los Angeles from Westwood is $3 one-way during the rush hour, commuters could reduce their costs 50 percent by simply traveling with two commuters per car.

One problem that runs throughout these market solutions is the effect they would have on the poor. In such cases as the deregulation of surface and local transportation markets, the poor would benefit directly and substantially in terms of lower prices and more easily available transportation. In the case of freeway pricing, Ward Elliot argues that the poor would be no worse off than under the current system.[43] Moreover, peak-load freeway drivers enjoy "about $400 a year worth of hidden subsidies, compared with $100 a year in open subsidies for bus riders." In short, some of the arguments against market pricing on the grounds of protecting the poor are probably fatuous.

In summary, these innovative market-oriented proposals no doubt have many shortcomings. They are advanced only to illustrate the main point about obstacles in the way of realizing the energy opportunities of the future. We shall probably not succeed in creating a future with abundant energy and a high quality of life unless we free ourselves from the constraints of corporate groupthink and governmental central planning and controls. The kind of innovation needed to create the energy future in which we would like our children to live is likely to come about only as the result of the rekindling of the entrepreneurial spirit in an open and competitive marketplace of ideas, goods, capital, labor, and resources.

Ultimate Abundance?

In the very long run, there is good reason for optimism about the
supply of energy. In the midst of the energy crisis of 1973 and 1974,
it was easy to slip into pessimism by forgetting that the world economy ultimately operates on the laws of supply and demand. Eventually, increases in the price of a commodity bring a host of restoring
forces into play. The recent increase in the price of crude oil was so
dramatic that the restoring forces generated may not be felt for a
decade—but they will be felt.

To be more specific, the price increase will eventually trigger unprecedented activity in the exploration for new fossil fuel deposits,
unearthing enough to meet man's needs for another two decades.
The higher price will significantly alter the curve of rapidly increasing
consumption, and put a variety of other long-term forces into play:
national energy policies aimed at greater fuel economy, reduced consumption, or national self-sufficiency. Even if the energy research
and development programs do not result in immediate stores of new
energy, every step along the road toward practical solar energy conversion, controlled nuclear fusion, and similar innovations will increase the nervousness of those who sit atop the large, known reserves of petroleum. Eventually, these countries will be tempted to
unload large amounts at bargain prices while there is still some demand in the marketplace.

It may take several years for a country like the United States to
make the transition from passenger automobiles that average 10 miles
per gallon to those averaging 35 miles per gallon, but such a transition is clearly under way. And as more and more countries (England,
Norway, Mexico, China) become major petroleum producers, any
thought of an international cartel to maintain an artificially high
petroleum price will vanish. Increased mining and use of coal along
with a proliferation of nuclear reactors will further increase the availability of energy, even in the short term. It is with good reason that

more and more economists are writing of the coming energy glut.

In any one of at least a dozen technological areas, a breakthrough could occur at almost any time that would have the effect of significantly increasing the quantity of energy available relative to human needs. Controlled fusion is one of the more highly publicized examples of this sort, but there are numerous more probable candidates. For example, solar energy would begin to play a major role if any one of several developments occurred: (1) a more efficient solar collector at a moderate price; (2) an inefficient but very cheap solar collector; (3) an inexpensive transducer for the direct conversion of sunlight into electricity; or (4) the development of a portable high-capacity energy storage device that could effect a very profound change for the better in the efficiency with which energy is consumed.

No doubt, ultimate abundance is still in iffy proposition. But the factors most likely to turn *if* into *when* are high energy prices brought about by market pressures and the unconstrained imagination of American entrepreneurs.

The short-run future forecasted here is basically optimistic, and the normative long-run future described is equally sanguine. Nevertheless, we feel compelled to conclude this report with a caveat. Because there will be no short-term crisis, we fear that complacency may obviate the steps necessary to achieve the long-term abundance we forecast. Although energy will be readily available for the next decade, in the short run it is necessary to begin to change energy practices. Energy prices need to be greatly increased *now* if a long-term crisis is to be avoided. Unfortunately, by mid-1976, American consumers were being lulled into complacency by the relaxation of the OPEC cartel on oil prices and were again wasting electricity in their homes, buying big cars, and joyriding. Many industries were becoming sloppy again in their conservation policies. Most distressing, the administration had backed off from its former proposals to deregulate and raise energy prices.

Although a Quality Economy of abundance is an "iffy" proposition, complacency is the factor most likely to lead to an economy of scarcity in the long run.

5. Results of the Delphi Study

Technological Forecasts

	Median responses indicating year by which there is a probability of		
	10%	50%	90%
1. The introduction of nonfossil, fully synthetic hydrogen-based automotive fuels on a commercial scale.	1992	2010	2025
2. The first placing into operation of a commercial electric power plant based on controlled thermonuclear fusion.	1991	2010	2025
3. The year by which there will be a technological breakthrough leading to the introduction of portable high-energy density sources of electricity that are acceptable with respect to cost, safety, and user convenience.	1981	1989	1998
4. The year by which there will be a technological breakthrough leading to the introduction of portable high-power density sources of electricity that are acceptable with respect to cost, safety, and user convenience.	1985	1990	1998
5. A technological breakthrough leading to the commercial production of synthetic food.	1980	1990	2000
6. The issuance of strict and enforceable federal regulations that reduce air and water pollution by at least 50 percent compared to 1974 standards.	1985	1993	2000
7. The year by which the daily production of oil from shale in the United States will begin to exceed 250,000 barrels.	1982	1990	1995

Note: The Delphi study was conducted in three rounds between November 1974 and March 1975.

	Median estimate for the year		
	1975	1985	1995
8. The percentage of U.S. electricity generated through atomic fission in the years 1975, 1985, and 1995.	8	25	40
9. The percentage of U.S. electric energy generated by solar power plants.	0	0.3	1
10. The percentage of U.S. electricity generated by coal.	41.5	40	38
11. The percentage of U.S. electricity generated through water power.	14	9	6.5
12. The percentage of U.S. electricity generated from oil or gas.	40	25	10
13. The degree of success of Project Independence, measured in terms of the percentage of U.S. energy consumption met by domestic energy production.	80	81	90
14. The percentage of petroleum used for nonenergy-producing purposes in the United States.	8	15	20
15. The degree of environmental pollution in the United States, measured on a scale from 0 (no pollution) to 100 (extinction of all forms of life), with the 1973 level of that degree set arbitrarily at 25.	25	20	10
16. The global amount of mineral-ore resources known at a given time that are commercially exploitable with the then-current technology (using an index value of 100 for 1973).	100	105	100
17. The global per capita food supply, measured on a scale from 0 (no food) to 100 (abundant food for everyone),			

	Median estimate for the year		
	1975	1985	1995
with the 1973 level of that index set arbitrarily at 50 and the level at which the annual death rate from starvation would be 1 percent set arbitrarily at 25.	50	40	50
18. The total amount of energy consumption in the United States, using an index value of 100 for the year 1973.	106	145	180
19. The amount of electric energy consumption in the United States, using an index value of 100 for the year 1973. (1965: 71; 1970: 82)	107	170	230
20. The annual amount of federal funding of research and development for opening up new energy sources in millions of 1973 dollars. (1965: 221; 1970: 295; 1973: 672)	800	1,600	2,500
21. The annual requirement of the U.S. energy industry for capital investment within the United States (in billions of 1973 dollars).	30	60*	100*
22. The percentage of coal in the United States produced by surface mining in the years 1975, 1985, 1995.	50	55	60
23. The total amount of electric energy produced in the United States, using an index value of 100 for 1973.	110	180	253
24. The total amount of energy (fuel and electric) consumed by U.S. industry, using an index value of 100 for 1973.	100	145	200

*There was considerable dissensus on the figures for 1985 and 1995.

	Median estimate for the year		
	1975	1985	1995
25. The percentage of total energy that *could be* saved through recycling in the United States.	10	10	10
26. The percentage of total energy that *will be* saved through recycling in the United States.	2	5	6

27. The subparts of this question inquired into the likelihood, timing, and nature of government regulations regarding such matters as strip-mining, offshore drilling, and industrial pollution and into the effect of such regulations on the supply and consumption of energy.

---

a. Though the short-range problem is one of energy supply, the long-range one is environmental in nature. Government regulations, therefore, can be expected to become less stringent during the next ten years and more stringent after ten years.   Consensus: Agree

---

b. A coherent governmental energy policy will not be developed in the next ten years.   Consensus: Agree

---

c. In about 10 years, the question of strip-mining will become academic, since the prospects are excellent for the development of in-situ recovery techniques such as coal gasification.   Consensus: Disagree

---

d. Coal will become an increasing source of energy in the United States during the next two decades.   Consensus: Agree

---

e. Government regulations will cause a 20 to 30 percent reduction in domes-

tic energy supply and create a delay in
energy growth in 6 to 19 months. Regulations will cause a 10 to 30 percent
increase in energy cost which in turn
will lead to a reduction in energy con-
sumption by 10 to 20 percent.   Consensus: Agree

f. Existing regulations concerning industrial pollution will be more rigo-
rously enforced than at present, espe-
cially with regard to water.   Consensus: Agree

g. Governmental regulations regarding
strip-mining, offshore drilling, and industrial pollution will be eased if the
energy shortage becomes more severe.   Consensus: Agree

h. Some government regulations will
be replaced by alternative forms of
control (such as pressure citizen groups
like Common Cause), which will become an important third element in
corporate accountability.   Consensus: Disagree

Economic Forecasts

	Median responses indicating year in which there is a probability of		
	10%	50%	90%
1. Legislation establishing the U.S. petroleum industry as a public utility or else nationalizing it altogether.	1978	1990	After 2050 if at all
2. A deterioration in the power of the OPEC to the point where it is no longer able to control petroleum prices.	1976	1980	1985
3. A serious breakdown in the world economic system, characterized by worldwide depression leading to drastic curtailments in the free flow of goods, services, and money among nations and creating conditions at least comparable in severity to those in 1931.	1977	Never	Never
4. The enactment of a federal truth-in-energy law.	1976	1977	1980

5. The annual increase in energy con-	Period		Period	
sumption in the United States com-	1975-1985		1985-1990	
pared to the increase in GNP. Specifi-	GNP growth rate		GNP growth rate	
cally, the average annual rate of in-	1%	3%	1%	3%
crease in energy consumption if the	1.15	2.67	1.25	2.75
average annual rate of increase in real (constant-dollar) GNP is 1 percent or 3 percent.				

a. The rates of increase in energy consumption, as estimated above would be *higher* if

(1) the price of energy were lowered;   Consensus: Agree

(2) a new political party were established;		Consensus: Disagree	
(3) there were a greater than anticipated relaxation of environmental controls.		Consensus: Agree	

b. The rates of increase in energy consumption, as estimated above would be *lower* if			
(1) the price of energy were raised;		Consensus: Agree	
(2) restrictive regulations on energy use were issued;		Consensus: Agree	
(3) technological breakthroughs were to lead to higher efficiency in energy use;		Consensus: Agree	
(4) transportation were replaced on a sizable scale by electronic communication.		Consensus: Agree	

	Median estimate for the year		
	1975	1985	1995
6. The annual growth rate of the population of the United States.	0.7%	0.6%	0.5%
7. The annual growth rate in real GNP of the United States.	1.1	3.0	3.0
8. The annual rate of inflation in the United States, based on the Consumer Price Index.	10	5	5
9. The international price of a barrel of crude oil, based on U.S. import prices, in constant 1973 dollars. (1965: $2.48; 1970: $2.30; 1973: $2.85)	10.25	7.68	10.00

10. The cost of energy in the United States, based on a deflated Consumer Price Index for fuel and utilities and

| | Median estimate for the year | | |
	1975	1985	1995
using an index value of 100 for 1973. (Trend data: 1965: 109; 1970: 97)	140	151	165*
11. The cost of labor, based on a deflated Wholesale Price Index for average hourly earnings of nonagricultural workers, using an index value of 100 for 1973. (Trend data: 1965: 88; 1970: 101)	107	120	140
12. The cost of food, based on a deflated Consumer Price Index for food, using an index value of 100 for 1973. (Trend data: 1965: 94; 1970: 93)	120	130	140
13. The cost of industrial raw materials (other than fuel), based on a deflated Wholesale Price Index for intermediate materials, supplies, and components, using an index value of 100 for 1973. (Trend data: 1965: 107; 1970: 107)	120	130	152
14. The percentage of all passenger transportation miles to and from work in the United States that is represented by private automobiles.	85	81	75
15. The amount of foreign investment in U.S. corporations, using an index value of 100 for 1973.	110	125	140
16. Estimates of the elasticity of energy demand in the United States as a function of price of energy, using an index value of 100 for the current energy demand, and assuming that the price were	a. *halved*, the demand would be 120; b. *doubled*, the demand would be 80; c. *tripled*, the demand would be 70.		

*No consensus reached on this item.

17. The percentage by which the cost
of energy would have to increase to
cause consumers to invest substantially in energy-saving home improve-
ments.   Median: 45%

a. From the consumers' point of view,
there may be a trade-off with regard to
home appliances between a higher initial purchase price and higher annual
operating costs. More precisely, if a
higher initial purchase price for energy-saving home appliances were expected to be amortized in x years
through savings in operating costs,
how small would x have to be to cause
substantial numbers of consumers to
buy such energy-saving appliances?   Median: 3 years

18. In answer to the question "how
the demand for energy in the United
States would be affected by shortages
in raw materials (other than petroleum
or food)—for instance, whether it
would be decreased because fewer
goods could be manufactured, or increased because of the difficulty in
either extracting minerals from lower
grade ores or replacing them with substitute materials"—there was a strong
consensus that the demand would increase in the long run, with the possibility of a slight decrease in the short
run.

19. The question asked for forecasts
concerning how the degree of energy
availability (shortage or abundance)
will affect the production of goods
and services in the United States.

a. Assume energy to be scarce; to be
specific, assume that the supply can
meet only 80 percent of the demand
at prices controlled at today's level. In
that case, by what percentage would
the real dollar value of the production
of goods and services be reduced?   Consensus: 10%

b. Under the same conditions, give
your opinion as to whether the replacement of capital by labor would
be negligible, slight, or considerable.   Consensus: Slight

c. Assume energy to be abundant; to
be specific, assume that there is a virtually perfectly elastic supply of energy at half of today's prices. In that
case, by what percentage would the
real dollar value of the production of
goods and services be increased?   Consensus: 10%

d. Under the same conditions, give
your opinion as to whether the replacement of labor by capital would
be negligible, slight, or considerable.   Consensus: Slight

20. The subparts of this question inquired into how the degree of energy
availability might affect institutional
aspects of business operations.

**I. Under the assumption of great
energy scarcity:**

a. The formation of cartels would be
slightly encouraged.   Consensus: Agree

b. Vertical integration would be
slightly favored over horizontal inte-
gration.   Consensus: Agree

c. An effect would be to increase the
formation and strength of consumer

groups.	Consensus: Agree
d. Bureaucracies would be expanded to administer controls.	Consensus: Agree

II. Under the assumption of great energy abundance:

a. The formation of cartels would be slightly discouraged.	Consensus: Agree
b. There would be little effect on the dollar volume of the business of multinational corporations.	Consensus: Agree
c. There would be essentially no effect on the formation of multinational corporations.	Consensus: Agree
d. There would be essentially no advantage of horizontal over vertical integration.	Consensus: Agree
e. There would be essentially no effect on unions.	Consensus: Agree
f. There would be essentially no effect on consumer groups.	Consensus: Agree
g. There would be less pressure for regulations and government intervention.	Consensus: Agree
h. The ecology and environment movement would be strengthened.	Consensus: Agree

21. The subparts of this question inquired into how much energy availability may affect the regulation of the production of goods and services.

I. Under the assumption of great energy scarcity:

a. The tendency toward nationalization of some business sectors would be encouraged.	Consensus: Agree

b. The amount of regulation of the exchange of goods would be slightly increased.	Consensus: Agree
c. The formation of regulatory agencies for dealing with specific problems such as pollution would be slightly encouraged.	Consensus: Disagree
d. The regulation of multinational corporations would be slightly increased.	Consensus: Agree
e. Allocations would increasingly become the subject of political debate.	Consensus: Agree
f. There would be more vigorous antitrust actions.	Consensus: Agree
II. Under the assumption of great energy abundance:	
a. The tendency toward nationalization of some business sectors would be strongly encouraged.	Consensus: Disagree
b. The formation of new regional governments would essentially not be affected.	Consensus: Agree
c. The formation of regulatory agencies for dealing with specific problems such as pollution would be slightly encouraged.	Consensus: Agree
d. The regulation of multinational corporations would essentially not be affected.	Consensus: Agree
e. Free enterprise would be encouraged.	Consensus: Agree
f. Environmental concerns would be encouraged and regulations will increase.	Consensus: Agree

22. The panel was asked the probability of a redistribution of power and status resulting in the emergence of a new elite under the assumptions of energy scarcity and energy abundance. Listed below are groups that might emerge as new elites, with the panel's opinion under each of the assumptions about the degree to which the power and status of these groups would be

strongly diminished	(−2)
slightly diminished	(−1)
essentially unchanged	(0)
slightly enhanced	(+1)
strongly enhanced	(+2)

Candidates for a new elite	Energy Scarcity	Energy Abundance
Big business	0*	0*
Small business	0	0
Scientists	1 1/2	0
Black marketers	1	−1 1/4
National economic planners	2	0
Technologists	2	0
Oil-exporting nations	2	−2
Coal- and nuclear-based utilities	2	− 1/4
Political activists	1	0
Economists	1/2	0
International bankers	1*	0*
Environmental specialists	−1	1 1/2
Consumerist politicians	1*	1/4*
Intellectuals generally	0	0
Bureaucrats in control of allocations	2	−1

*No consensus reached on these items.

23. During the next few decades, nations may "specialize" to make the most of their resources and capabilities, even though this may increase their dependence on others. There will be a significant increase in such specialization.   Consensus: Disagree

Social Forecasts

Responses marked with a double aster-
isk (**) are based on median responses
of panelists on a standard seven-point
scale: for example,

1	2	3	4	5	6	7
Disagree strongly		Disagree		Agree		Agree strongly

All the forecasts in this section assume
energy scarcity.

---

1. The subparts of this question inquired into the possible effects of energy constraints on the nature of work
and work situations.

---

a. Production would become more
labor-intensive as energy scarcity becomes more acute. Decentralization
would thus become more efficient and
smaller enterprises would proliferate.
These smaller firms would tend to re-
duce the impersonality of work. | Consensus: Agree

---

b. Managers would be forced to dele-
gate authority and decentralize decision making at every level of operations simply to keep operations going.
Managers would thus be required to
understand how to manage discretion-
ary performance. | Consensus: Disagree

---

c. The wealth distribution impact of
the allocation of scarce energy via market pricing would be substantially different than via governmental rationing
of energy. | Consensus: Agree

---

2. In response to energy scarcity, the
strength of any reverse migration of
the educated middle class to the
central cities. | Consensus: No migration to
only moderate migration

---

3. The subparts of this question inquired into the possible effects of energy on bureaucratic structures.

a. If energy available for transporta- tion and other uses becomes increas- ingly scarce, it is probable that de- pendence on bureaucratic structures for decision making will increase.	Consensus: Agree
b. Allocation of scarce energy by mar- ket pricing mechanisms would be less likely to increase dependence on bureaucracies than would allocation by government rationing because mar- ket pricing tends to decentralize ener- gy use decisions to the individual level.	Consensus: Agree
c. In coping with energy scarcity, the strength of any shift in people's life- styles (substituting bicycles for cars, heating homes with individual solar units, growing vegetable gardens, pro- ducing backyard methane).	Consensus: Moderate shift**
d. If such individual responses to the scarcity of energy occur, there will be a diminished reliance on bureaucracy.	Consensus: Moderately disagree**
e. If bureaucratic decision making were to increase (as a consequence of energy scarcity), people's reliance on social middlemen (such as ombuds- men, consumer advocates, public re- view boards) would increase.	Consensus: Agree
f. Governmental rationing of scarce energy would encourage more middle- men (ombudsmen and consumer ad- vocates) than would market pricing, because pricing would decentralize energy use decisions to a greater degree.	Consensus: Agree**

g. In the event that market pricing
mechanisms were used to allocate
scarce energy, this would be less likely
to lead to bureaucracy than would
government rationing.   Consensus: Moderately agree**

h. If free market-pricing mechanisms
(rather than governmental controls)
were used to allocate scarce energy
resources, the process would quickly
raise income allocation problems and,
therefore, would require government
intervention.   Consensus: Agree

i. If government controls were used
(rather than free market mechanisms),
this might restrict the ability of organizations to respond to changing condi-
tions.   Consensus: Agree

j. Under the same conditions, greater
reliance on middlemen would be required who would concentrate on
problems related to bureaucratic procedures involved in enforcing alloca-
tion decisions.   Consensus: Agree

k. Under the same conditions, tenden-
cies toward bureaucratic decision mak-
ing and dependence would increase.   Consensus: Agree

4. Assuming energy scarcity, the probability that this will lead to an increase
in nearby neighborhood activities in
recreation, politics, work, education,
and commerce (shopping). Two estimates are given for each case, one for
a situation in which scarce energy is
allocated through pricing mechanisms,
the other through government controls.

	Probability of Increase	
	Median responses	
	Pricing	Controls
Recreation	80	70
Work	65	50
Commerce	75	70
Education	65	50
Politics	50	50

a. Assuming energy scarcity, government controls more than market pricing will result in more energy conservation because they will be invoked
when market pricing approaches fail
to achieve the desired ends.   Consensus: Agree

b. Government controls would curtail
luxury activities more than would mar-
ket pricing mechanisms.   Consensus: Agree[x][x]

c. Assuming energy scarcity, the major
impact both of government controls
and of market pricing would result
from costs and restrictions in the area
of transportation.   Consensus: Agree

d. Regarding education, recreation,
politics, and commerce, no major differences in locale of activity can be
expected as a consequence of the
choice between government controls
and market pricing.   Consensus: Moderately disagree[**]

e. In the education arena, market pricing will make more private alternatives
available to those with greater means,
while government controls will lead to
more across-the-board use of central-
ized local educational facilities.   Consensus: Agree[**]

5. The probability of an increase or decrease in the level of political participation on the part of the general public (possibly as a result of increased difficulty in satisfying personal needs due to a shortage of energy):	Median response
Probability of an increase	70.3%
Probability that the level will remain essentially the same	24.3%
Probability of decrease	5.4%
(Normalized to add up to 100)	

a. Energy uses and impacts are so pervasive and diverse that it will be ex-

tremely difficult to organize viable
political factions around any particular energy issue, and thus political
activity on the part of the general pub-
lic is likely to decrease.   Consensus: Disagree

b. Though energy shortages may stimulate an increase in political behavior,
the general public has become so cynical and alienated by politics in recent
years that its level of political participation is likely to decline further as
the shortages make even clearer to individuals that they are progressively
losing control over their own destinies.   Consensus: Disagree

c. Energy shortages will impinge so
closely on personal affairs that members of the general public are likely to
participate increasingly in politics to
alleviate their circumstances.   Consensus: Agree

6. The subparts of this question inquired into the possible effects of energy scarcity on such family life-styles
as communes, childless marriages, and
common-law marriages.

a. Unconventional family life-styles
(communes, childless marriages, common-law marriages) would not be
greatly influenced by energy scarcities.   Consensus: Moderately agree**

b. Any increase in the variety of family life-styles that may be fostered by
a scarcity of energy is not likely to be
affected by whether the allocative
process involves market pricing or
government controls.   Consensus: Agree

c. The impact of market pricing might
seem a little more rapid, wild, and out
of control, and thereby increase the

probability of breaks with traditional
life styles.   Consensus: Disagree

7. Assuming a scarcity of energy, the		Median response
probability that there will be substantial changes in the nature or size of public and private institutions that will affect the freedom of individuals.	Probability, if allocation of scarce energy is through market pricing:	70%
	Probability, if allocation is through government rationing:	80%

a. The expansion of governmental regulation of energy-use decisions would threaten the individual's experience of this society as free (as one that does not constrain him).   Consensus: Moderately disagree**

8. The subparts of this question inquired into the probabilities of large-scale social upheaval in response to governmental actions undertaken to curb energy use.

a. Americans are not likely to opt for major social upheavals in reaction to social controls (imposed to accomplish broadly perceived social goods).   Consensus: Agree**

b. Social upheaval would occur only if people became aware of gross unfairness or became subject to totalitarian measures.   Consensus: Agree strongly**

c. Explosive forms of polarization to the right and left would increase through decades of energy restrictions that cause reallocations of power and wealth.   Consensus: Moderately agree**

d. Severe economic problems always motivate people strongly, particularly when the contrast with prior affluence makes conditions intolerable. Economically disadvantaged groups

that have least to lose—ethnic minori-
ties—could become militant.   Consensus: Agree**

e. Unlike the experience of the 1930s,
more recent experience indicates that
people are learning that violence
works.   Consensus: Agree

9. The subparts of this question inquired into the probable effects of
scarcities other than of energy (such
as food or raw materials).

a. Most scarcity problems are interlinked. The most disruptive in all cases
would be food shortages, because food
affects a more basic need level than
other scarcities.   Consensus: Agree

b. Food shortages would probably increase citizen dissatisfaction with institutional managements (government
or private) faster than other scarcities.   Consensus: Agree

c. Food shortages would encourage
high organizational, social, and cultural dissonance as well as high political
involvement.   Consensus: Agree

d. Raw material shortages are likely to
have delayed effects (because of their
relatively slow flow to consumers,
many being used primarily for capital
development) and much more selective
effects (in terms of citizens' feeling of
discomfort).   Consensus: Agree

10. Political opposition to pricing
mechanisms for the allocation of energy would be greatly reduced if taxes
and transfer payments were adjusted
to mitigate the effects on lower and
middle classes.   Consensus: Agree**

Political and International Forecasts

1. The subparts of this question inquired into the probability that conditions of energy availability would lead nations to surrender substantial sovereignty to a new or revitalized world organization (such as the United Nations).

a. There will be an increase in international organizations (consumer blocks) but no significant surrender of national sovereignty as a result of energy problems.	Consensus: Agree
b. A severe energy shortage (if OPEC cut back oil production by at least 10 percent for a lengthy period) would lead to a substantial surrender of sovereignty.	Consensus: Disagree
c. The probability of a worldwide surrender of sovereignty occurring by 1995.	Median response: 15%

2. The subparts of this question inquired into the kinds of regional or shared-interest supranational organizations likely to be formed in coming years in response to recognition of the increasing interdependence of nations (such organizations as OPEC or the European Common Market).

a. The following kinds of regional or shared-interest supranational groups are likely or unlikely to be formed in coming years in response to recognition of the increasing interdependence of nations (suggested by Delphi Panel).	Oil consumer organization World Food Bank Regional blocs around powerful neighbors Ocean resources management organization Strengthened International Monetary Fund or IMF-type organization to

recycle oil funds
Raw materials cartels for things like
    tin, sugar, bauxite, iron, etc.
No world resource management board

---

b. The importance of energy availability as a factor in the forming of such
organizations, on a scale of 1 (central
factor) to 10 (not a factor at all).   Median response: 6

---

3. The probability of another Arab-
Israeli war.

	Distribution of responses		
Probability in the Years	Lower quartile	Median	Upper quartile
1975-1980	70%	80%	99%
1980-1985	20%	35%	72%

---

4. The probability that there will be
another Arab oil embargo.

	Distribution of responses		
Probability in the Years	Lower quartile	Median	Upper quartile
1975-1980	60%	70%	80%
1980-1985	20%	30%	50%

---

5. The probability of consumer nations
taking military actions to achieve control of oil supplies.

	Distribution of responses		
Probability in the Years	Lower quartile	Median	Upper quartile
1975-1980	10%	20%	40%
1980-1985	0%	15%	40%

---

6. A national energy policy will be an-
nounced shortly, but it will be unclear
and ineffective.   Consensus: Agree

---

a. If a national energy policy were to   Price supports for domestic producers
come in any form it would likely have   Accelerated support for fusion pro-
the following characteristics (suggested   grams
by Delphi Panel).   Tax on excessive consumption
                                               Development of solar, geothermal,
                                                   methane and other secondary sources

	Heavy reliance on research and development Increase in domestic production of oil, gas, uranium, and coal Reduction of environmental standards
b. If a policy comes, it is *unlikely* to have the following characteristics:	Rationing of gasoline A deal with China or other country to break oil cartel

Dissensus Items

At the conclusion of the three Delphi rounds, the panel's responses were widely divergent for a number of questions. As expected, such dissensus was found most often among those social and political questions that least lent themselves to quantitative measurement. We feel that dissensus should not be interpreted as a failure of the panel or of the Delphi method. Rather, dissensus helps to identify issues on which expert opinion is widely divided as a result of the complex nature of the issue at hand, ideological differences, or different views of social process. (In some cases, of course, the dissensus was the result of confusing wording of questions. Where this obviously occurred, we have eliminated these questions from this report.)

1. The average efficiency of energy utilization in the United States.	Median estimate for the year		
	1975	1985	1995
	30	45	42
	Note: There was considerable dissensus on the actual figures for 1985 and 1995. However, there was considerable agreement that the percentage increase over 1975 would average about 5 percent every ten years.		

2. The percentage probability that rationing of electric energy or of petroleum for industrial use (such as occurred during World War II) will be imposed.	Median estimates for the years		
	1975-1980	1980-1985	1985-1990
	22.5%	22.5%	17.5%

3. Under the assumption of great energy *scarcity*, estimates of the effect on the dollar volume of the business of multinational corporations:	3 respondents forecast lower dollar volume. 4 respondents forecast higher dollar volume. 5 respondents forecast little effect (although possibly in different composition).

4. Under the assumption of great energy *scarcity*, estimates of the effect on union activities:	4 respondents forecast that such activities would be encouraged. 2 respondents forecast that such activities would be discouraged. 6 respondents forecast that there would be little effect.

5. Under the assumption of great energy *scarcity*, the formation of new regional governments essentially would *not* be affected:	6 panelists agreed. 4 panelists disagreed.

6. Under the assumption of great energy *abundance*, the amount of regulation of the exchange of goods and services would be slightly diminished:	6 panelists agreed. 4 panelists disagreed.
7. Price mechanisms for allocating energy would lead to a more rapid shift to labor-intensive activities than would governmental rationing:	Panel responses were spread fairly evenly along a scale of 1 (strongly disagree) to 7 (strongly agree).
8. In the event that government rationing were used to allocate scarce energy, this would be more likely than would pricing mechanisms to lead to a fair allocation of energy:	Responses were divergent, but were skewed toward agreement with the statement.
9. In the areas of recreation, work, and commerce, a government control approach more than a market-pricing approach will lead to greater use of local, neighborhood facilities:	On a scale of 1 (strongly disagree) to 7 (strongly agree) responses skewed slightly toward disagreement.
10. Under the market pricing scenario as compared to government controls, we can expect more adherence to the status quo with respect to localization of activities:	Responses spread rather evenly across scale, only marginally skewed toward disagreement.
11. Of the five areas of education, recreation, politics, work, and commerce, we can expect the least impact of decreased energy resources to be in the political area:	Responses spread rather evenly across scale.

12. Our country is currently witnessing an increase in the variety of family life-styles (such as communes, childless marriages, common-law marriages) that purportedly represent a break with our social traditions. Assuming a scarcity of energy, the probability that these family styles will become at least twice as common as they are now:

	Median responses
Probability, if allocation of scarce energy is through market pricing:	55
Probability, if allocation is through government rationing:	45

Responses ranged from 0 percent to 100 percent.

13. Assuming governmental actions being undertaken to curb energy use, the probability of large-scale social upheaval in response to such policies:	Median estimate: 40 percent. Responses ranged from 0 percent to 100 percent.
14. High prices and high profits would be more likely than scarcities of energy, food, or other commodities to lead to violent social or political upheaval:	Responses were widely divergent.
15. The subparts of this question inquired into the conditions of energy availability or other international political or economic developments that would lead nations to surrender substantial sovereignty to a new or revitalized world organization (such as the United Nations).	
a. There are no probable conditions under which nations will surrender substantial sovereignty:	10 panelists agreed. 7 panelists disagreed.
b. There will be even less international cooperation in the future because scarcities tend to strengthen nationalism and the unwillingness of haves to share with have-nots:	10 panelists agreed. 8 panelists disagreed.
c. Only a world war or a series of serious regional wars would lead to a surrender of sovereignty to a world organization:	8 panelists agreed. 9 panelists disagreed.
d. Nations will surrender substantial sovereignty if there is a severe scarcity of food brought about, for example, by a radical shift in worldwide climate patterns:	9 panelists agreed. 9 panelists disagreed.

| e. A substantial surrender of sovereignty would occur if the flow of money to oil producers leads to a worldwide economic collapse: | 8 panelists agreed. 10 panelists disagreed. |

16. New kinds of regional or shared-interest supranational organizations likely to be formed in coming years in response to recognition of increasing interdependence of nations (organizations such as the OPEC oil cartel or the European Common Market):		Agree	Disagree
	International police force to deal with terrorists	8	9
	Food producers' cartel	11	6
	World petroleum organization, comprised of producer and consumer nations	10	7
	Resource-user cartels or consumer co-ops	11	6

17. A strong, clear national energy policy will be enunciated by the year		1976	1978	1980	1984	Not before 1985
	Panelists' responses:	3	1	7	2	5

18. If a national energy policy comes, and in whatever form, it would likely have the following characteristics:		Agree	Disagree
	Governmental partnership with industry	8	11
	Increased reliance on mass transit	12	6
	Cooperation with other consuming nations	8	10

Delphi Technology Panel

Elmer Dougherty
Petroleum Engineering Department
University of Southern California

Harry Gately
Planning Analyst
Sears, Roebuck & Company
Chicago, Illinois

Theodore Gordon
The Futures Group
Glastonbury, Connecticut

Robert Hellwarth
Physics and Electrical Engineering
Departments
University of Southern California

Albert R. Hibbs
Jet Propulsion Laboratory
Pasadena, California

George A. Hoffman
Systems Engineering Department
University of Southern California

Young B. Kim
Physics and Electrical Engineering
Departments
University of Southern California

S. W. Kingsbury
Atlantic Richfield Company
Los Angeles, California

M. E. Kirkpatrick
TRW, Incorporated
Redondo Beach, California

Seymour Lampert
Safety and Systems Management
Department
University of Southern California

E. Stanley Lee
Chemical and Electrical Engineering
Departments
University of Southern California

Frank Lehan
Technologist
Montecito, California

Jacques Maroni
Energy Planning Manager
Ford Motor Company
Dearborn, Michigan

Deane Morris
The Rand Corporation
Santa Monica, California

John R. Pierce
California Institute of Technology
Pasadena, California

Chauncey Starr
Electric Power Research Institute
Palo Alto, California

William Van Vorst
School of Engineering
University of California at Los Angles

Philip C. White
General Manager of Research
Standard Oil Company (Indiana)
Chicago, Illinois

Ian Wilson
Business Environment Research
General Electric Company
Fairfield, Connecticut

Delphi Economic Panel

Kazem Attaran, Economist
Division of Transportation Planning
California Department of
Transportation
Sacramento, California

Robert Barmeier
Director, Office of Planning and
Research
Sears, Roebuck & Company
Chicago, Illinois

Thomas H. Bates
School of World Business
San Francisco State University

Harry Biederman
Development Planning Division
Lockheed Aircraft Corporation
Burbank, California

Patrick M. Boarman
Monex International
Newport Beach, California

David Clark
Dean of Research and Graduate
Studies
Portland University
Portland, Oregon

Theodore R. Eck, Chief Economist
Standard Oil Company (Indiana)
Chicago, Illinois

W. D. Hermann
Bechtel Corporation
San Francisco, California

Michael Intriligator
Economics Department
University of California at Los Angeles

William Iulo
Economics Department
Washington State University
Pullman, Washington

Neil Jacoby
School of Management
University of California at Los Angeles

G. E. Medin
Manager, Planning Services
Atlantic Richfield Company
Los Angeles, California

Jeffrey Nugent
Economics Department
University of Southern California

Edward Rubin
Action Programs International
Santa Monica, California

Lester C. Thurow
Massachusetts Institute of Technology
Cambridge, Massachusetts

Whitney S. Wilson
Business Analysis Staff of Systems
and Energy
TRW, Incorporated
Redondo Beach, California

Delphi Social Panel

Marvin Adelson
School of Architecture and Urban
Planning
University of California at Los Angeles

Wendell Bell
Department of Sociology
Yale University
New Haven, Connecticut

Harvey Cox
Divinity School
Harvard University
Cambridge, Massachusetts

John Dyckman
Urban and Regional Planning
University of Southern California

Ward Edwards
Social Science Research Institute
University of Southern California

Amitai Etzioni
Center for Policy Research, Inc.
New York, New York

Marcia Guttentag
Department of Social Ethics
Harvard University
Cambridge, Massachusetts

Hazel Henderson
Social Critic
Public Interest Economic Center
Princeton, New Jersey

William R. Herman
National Governor's Conference
Washington, D.C.

Thomas Mandel
Stanford Research Institute
Menlo Park, California

Martin E. Marty
Divinity School
The University of Chicago
Chicago, Illinois

David C. Miller
DCM Associates
San Francisco, California

S. M. Miller
Sociology Department
Boston University
Boston, Massachusetts

Dorothy K. Newman
An American Dilemma Revisited
Washington, D.C.

John Platt
University of Michigan
Ann Arbor, Michigan

S. Prakash Sethi
Graduate School of Business
University of California at Berkeley

Notes

Notes to Chapter 1

1. Lynn White, *Medieval Technology and Social Change* (New York: Oxford University Press, 1962).

2. Ibid., p. 38.

3. Ibid., pp. 41-45.

4. Ibid., pp. 70-78.

5. Ibid., p. 28.

6. Ibid., p. 88.

7. Ibid., p. 134.

8. Lynn White, "The Historical Roots of Our Ecological Crisis," *Science*, 155 (March 10, 1967): 1203-1207.

9. Philip Gram, "The Energy Crisis in Perspective," *Wall Street Journal* (November 30, 1973), p. 8.

10. Morley English, "The Long-Run Price of Energy Will Be Down," (Los Angeles: paper commissioned by the University of Southern California for the report, 1974).

11. Robert Heilbroner, *The Future as History*, New York: Harper and Row, 1960. In this important book, Heilbroner introduced the concept of future shock some ten years before it was popularized by Alvin Toffler.

12. David MacMichael, "Future Studies and Historical Method" (unpublished paper, Stanford Research Institute), p. 4.

13. Ibid., p. 1.

14. Ibid., p. 5.

Notes to Chapter 2

1. Hugo Pomrehn, "Technical Forecast of Energy Systems 1970-2020" (Ph.D. diss., University of Southern California, 1975), Sec. 2.2, pp. 1-2.

2. Ibid., pp. 2-3.

3. E. Cooke, "The Flow of Energy in an Industrial Society," *Scientific American*, 225, no. 3 (September 1971): 136.

4. C. Starr, "Energy and Power," *Scientific American*, 225, no. 3 (September 1971): 40.

5. Pomrehn, *Technical Forecast*.

6. Ibid., p. 5.

7. Ibid.

8. H. Linden, "Energy Self-Sufficiency: A Look at the Future," *The Future Is Now* (Los Angeles: Council of Engineers and Scientists Proceedings Series, April 1975), p. 31.

9. Ibid., p. 33.

10. Efficiency could be expected to decrease with an increase in the cost of energy because technologies designed on the assumption of "cheap energy" could not be quickly replaced, and this would prevent industries using these technologies from conserving fuel.

11. The data may also somewhat reflect the cost of pollution control.

12. Ironically, while using these price-lowering policies with one hand the government was using import quotas with the other, which had a countereffect on prices.

13. Edward Mitchell, *U.S. Energy Policy: A Primer* (Washington, D.C.: American Enterprise Institute, 1974), p. 82.

14. E. F. Schumacher, *Small Is Beautiful: Economics As If People Mattered*, (New York: Harper and Row, 1975), p. 131.

15. Charles J. Ryan, "Energy: The New First Estate," in *Energy: Today's Choices, Tomorrow's Opportunities* ed. Anton B. Schmalz (Washington, D.C.: World Future Society, 1974), p. 134.

16. Metropolitan Water District, 1941, 1973. As quoted in English, "The Long-Run Price," p. 13.

17. Ibid., p. 13.

18. Wilson Clark, *Energy for Survival: The Alternative for Extinction* (New York: Anchor Books, 1974). As quoted in English, "The Long-Run Price," p. 13.

19. English, "The Long-Run Price," p. 14.

20. David Pimental, "Food Production and the Energy Crisis," *Science*, 182 (November 2, 1973): 96.

21. Ibid., pp. 98-99.

22. John Steinhart and Carol Steinhart, "Energy Use in the U.S. Food System," *Science*, 184 (April 19, 1974): 307-308.

23. Ryan, "Energy: The New First Estate," p. 135.

24. Stewart Udall, Charles Conconi, and David Osterhout, *The Energy Balloon* (New York: McGraw-Hill, 1974).

Notes to Chapter 3

1. Edward Teller, *Energy: A Plan for Action* (New York: Commission on Critical Choices for Americans, 1975), p. 7.

2. Dall W. Forsythe, "An Energy-Scarce Society: The Politics and Possibilities," *Working Papers*, 2, no. 1 (Spring 1974): 3-12.

3. Les Gapay, "Weighing All the Energy Options," *Wall Street Journal* (December 13, 1974), p. 12.

4. Ford Foundation, Energy Policy Project, *A Time To Choose* (Cambridge: Ballinger, 1974), pp. 135-136.

5. Should we believe the econometricians' or the experts' opinions? A recent *Fortune* article indicates that the judgmental forecasts of economists have, on the average, been more reliable than econometric forecasts using complex computer models of the economy. Deborah Malley, "Lawrence Klein and his Forecasting Machine," *Fortune*, 91, no. 3 (March 1975): 153-157.

6. If a slightly lower GNP growth rate is coupled with a declining birth rate, GNP per capita could retain its historical pattern for a decade or so.

7. Allen Mazur and Eugene Rosa, "Energy and Lifestyle," *Science*, 186 (November 15, 1974): 608-609.

8. The degree of dislocation, of course, varies with each industry's dependence on energy and the demand elasticities for their products.

9. Irving Kristol, "The Credibility of Corporations," *Wall Street Journal* (January 17, 1974), p. 4.

10. James O'Toole, "Lordstown Three Years Later," *Business and Society Review*, no. 13 (Spring 1975): 64-71.

11. In some highly automated plants, the depreciation of machinery is often a higher cost than the wages of labor.

12. Edison Electric Institute, *Questions and Answers About the Electric Utility Industry* (New York: Edison Electric Institute, 1973).

13. Selwyn Enzer, "Alternative Futures for California," (Los Angeles: University of Southern California, Center for Futures Research, 1975).

14. Stephen P. Taylor, "Financial Background for Project Independence," in *Energy, Profits and Taxation*, the American Petroleum Institute summary of petroleum industry witnesses appearing before the Senate Committee on Finance, February 14, 1974.

15. The Brookings estimates rest on the assumption of a "full-employment" surplus. *Capital Needs In The Seventies* (Washington, D.C.: Brookings Institution, 1975).

16. Wayne Clark, "Energy Industry Capital Expenditures Forecast" (Los Angeles: paper commissioned by the University of Southern California for the study, 1974), pp. 19-25.

17. Ford Foundation, *A Time To Choose*, p. 141.

18. David Ignatius has joined Milton Fried-

man and others in taking a jaundiced view of the "capital crisis" forecast by the New York Stock Exchange: "For starters, the very notion of a 'capital shortage' is absurd to any serious free-marketeer . . . there can be no 'shortage' of capital, since the rate of interest will always exactly balance the supply of savings and the demand for investment." David Ignatius, "The Capital Crisis: Crying Wolf on Wall Street," The Washington Monthly (November 1975), p. 19.

19. Walter Heller, "Taxes and the 'Capital Shortfall,'" Wall Street Journal (August 19, 1975).

20. Ford Foundation, A Time To Choose, p. 118.

21. These are offset to some degree, of course, by the cost-of-living indexing of social security benefits.

22. B. Bruce-Briggs, "Gasoline Prices and the Suburban Way of Life," The Public Interest, no. 37 (Fall 1974), p. 133.

23. John W. Dyckman, "Speculations of Future Urban Form" (unpublished report, the Center for Metropolitan Planning and Research, The Johns Hopkins University, no date), pp. A-4, A-5.

24. From Richard Coleman's unpublished "Social Standing in America" (Cambridge: MIT-Harvard Joint Center for Urban Studies, no date).

25. Daniel Yankelovich, "The Upturn: How Soon? How Strong?" Time (May 5, 1975), pp. 67-69.

26. Bertrand de Jouvenel, The Art of Conjecture (New York: Basic Books, 1967).

27. There is a great need, of course, to develop such techniques.

28. Jurgen Moultman, "Freedom in Time and Space," Religion, Revolution and the Future, trans. M. Douglas Meehs (New York: Scribner's, 1969).

29. Daniel Bell, "The Corporation in the 1970s," The Public Interest, no. 25 (Summer 1971): 5-33.

Notes to Chapter 4
1. Harrison Brown, The Challenge of Man's Future (New York: Viking, 1954), quoted in E. F. Schumacher, Small Is Beautiful (New York: Harper and Row, 1975).

2. Charles Berg, "Conservation in Industry," Science, 184, no. 4134 (April 19, 1974): 264-271.

3. Selwyn Enzer, Some Social Impacts of Alternative Energy Policies, (Menlo Park: Institute for the Future, 1975).

4. Kenneth Boulding, "The Social System and the Energy Crisis," Science, 184, no. 4134 (April 19, 1974): 255-257.

5. MIT Energy Laboratory Policy Study Group, Energy Self Sufficiency: An Economic Evaluation, National Energy Study 3 (Washington, D.C.: American Enterprise Institute, 1974).

6. English, "The Long-Run Price," pp. 34-36.

7. Robert Stobaugh, "The Hard Choices on Energy," Wall Street Journal (December 9, 1974), p. 22.

8. Russel E. Train, "The Long-Term Value of the Energy Crisis," The Futurist, 2, no. 1 (February 1973): 16.

9. This section is based on Enzer, Some Societal Impacts.

10. Oak Park, Illinois, was once heated this way.

11. This section is based on Selwyn Enzer, Alternative Futures for California, a report for the Center for Futures Research, University of Southern California (September 1975), F-22. By battery, we mean any high-density, high-powered energy storage device—including flywheels. Some efficient heat storage devices are already available. In Britain, many homes have storage heaters

that are cheaply warmed using off-peak electrical capacity. These storage devices are simple, bricklike substitutes that remain warm for as long as twenty-four hours.

12. W. Dale Compton, "Energy Conversion and Storage Technology—The Sodium-Sulfur Battery," in *Energy, Environment, Producitivity* (RAAN, National Science Foundation, 1974), pp. 25-26.

13. *Important for the Future* (United Nations Institute for Training and Research), 1, no. 1 (September 1975): 17.

14. This section on methanol is based on George Hoffman's "The U.S. Fuel Industry In The 21st Century," (Los Angeles: paper commissioned by the University of Southern California Center for Futures Research, 1974).

15. Ibid.

16. In Brazil, however, the government has just broken ground for the construction of a large methanol plant.

17. Certainly, methanol is not enough by itself to meet the nation's energy problems. But it probably will be necessary to aggregate many little solutions rather than put all our eggs in one basket. Adding incremental eggs to a pile will eventually make a big pile.

18. The technological continuum is an enlargement of the automation continuum discussed briefly in Edward E. Lawler and J. Richard Hackman, "Corporate Profits and Employee Satisfaction: Must They Be In Conflict?" *California Management Review*, 14, no. 1 (1971): 46-55. In some ways, this formulation may appear inconsistent with the concept recently exposed in E. F. Schumacher's *Small Is Beautiful: Economics As If People Mattered* (New York: Harper and Row, 1975). Most of the differences center on these points: Schumacher's constructs are designed for developing countries, whereas mine are suggested only for the United States; and Schumacher's "intermediate technologies" are, in the

main, low technology on my continuum.

19. Schumacher, *Small Is Beautiful*, pp. 151-152.

20. Ralph Knowles, "Urban Transformation: An Architect Looks at the Energy Problem," *Facets*, 1 (Spring 1975): 30.

21. Ibid., p. 33.

22. From Bill Hieronymus, "With a Nod to History and Energy Crisis, Many Firms Renovate Their Old Buildings," *Wall Street Journal* (January 2, 1975), p. 4.

23. Associated Press, February 16, 1975.

24. Pollution control can be profitable, according to Carl A. Gerstacker, chairman of the board of Dow Chemical. At one Dow silicon metal factory a $2.7 million investment to recover chemicals previously lost to the atmosphere returns $900,000 per year. Sylvia Porter, "Why We Can't Afford Smog," *San Francisco Chronicle* (November 14, 1975), p. 62.

25. Ford Foundation, *A Time To Choose*, p. 68.

26. Ted Bartell, "The Effects of the Energy Crisis on Attitudes and Lifestyles of Los Angeles Residents" (paper presented at 69th Annual Meeting of the American Sociological Association, August 26-29, 1974).

27. "Gallup Survey Finds 5% Drop In Use of Cars To Get To Work," *The New York Times* (February 16, 1975), p. 54.

28. Glenn Seaborg, "The Recycle Society," in *Energy: Today's Choices, Tomorrow's Opportunities* (Washington: World Future Society, 1974), p. 283.

29. Quoted in William J. Barger, "Will Scarcity of Energy Lead to Substitution of Labor for Capital?" (first four paragraphs of this section are based on Barger's paper, which was commissioned for this study).

30. Today, however, capital accounts for

only about 50 percent of the growth in
GNP.

31. James O'Toole, et al., *Work in America*
(Cambridge: MIT Press, 1973).

32. E. J. Mishan, "Ills, Bads, and Disamenities: The Wages of Growth," *Daedalus*
(1973), pp. 63-87.

33. Roger Bezdek and Bruce Hannon, "Energy, Manpower, and the Highway Trust
Fund," *Science*, 185 (August 23, 1974):
669-675.

34. Ibid.

35. Sylvia Porter argues that a $1 billion in-
vestment in sewer and treatment plants
creates 85,000 jobs, making this activity almost as labor-intensive as health care.

36. Mishan, "Ills, Bads, and Disamenities "

37. James O'Toole, "The Reserve Army of
the Underemployed," *Change* (May-June
1975).

38. Stewart Udall, Charles Conconi, and
David Osterhout, *The Energy Balloon* (New
York: McGraw Hill, 1974).

39. It is not bad that we import so many
ideas, of course, but it is bad that we produce so few.

40. *Ohio* v. *West Virginia*, 262, U.S. 544
(1923).

41. Daniel Kasper, Edmund Kitch, and
Marc Isaacson, "The Regulation of Taxicabs
in Chicago," *Journal of Law and Economics*,
14 (1971): 285-350.

42. Ward Elliot, "The Los Angeles Affliction: Suggestions for a Cure," *Public Interest*, no. 38 (Winter 1975): 125.

43. Ibid., p. 126.

Bibliography

Adams, F. Gerald, Griffin, James M., and Preston, Ross S. "The Energy Crisis: Short and Long Perspectives." *Wharton Quarterly*, Spring 1974, pp. 20-24.

Adams, James R. "Bringing OPEC to the Bar." *Wall Street Journal*, May 20, 1975, p. 22.

Adelman, Morris A., Jacoby, Henry D., Joskow, Paul L., MacAvory, Paul W., Meissner, Herman P., White, David C., Zimmerman, Martin, B. "Energy Self-Sufficiency: An Economic Evaluation." *Technology Review*, May 1974, pp. 23-58.

_____. *The World Oil Market*. Baltimore: The Johns Hopkins University Press, 1973.

Aliber, Robert Z. "Impending Breakdown of OPEC Cartel." *Wall Street Journal*, March 20, 1975, p. 22.

"America's Mountain of Debt." *Plain Truth*, 40, no. 19 (November 22, 1975): 4.

American Enterprise Institute. *National Energy Project*. Dialogue on World Oil. Highlights of a conference on world oil problems. Washington, D.C.: American Enterprise Institute, 1974.

_____. *The Energy Crisis. Proceedings* of one of a series of AEI Round Table Discussions. Washington, D.C.: American Enterprise Institute, 1974.

_____. *Is the Energy Crisis Contrived? Proceedings* of one of a series of AEI Round Table Discussions. Washington, D.C.: American Enterprise Institute, 1974.

Arnold, Bob. "Energy Alternatives: Gas and Oil From Coal Can Help Us Overcome U.S. Fuel Shortage." *Wall Street Journal*, May 3, 1974, p. 1.

Arthur D. Little, Inc. *FEA Draft Report on Capital Needs and Federal Policy*, August, 1974.

Barger, William J. "Will Scarcity of Energy Lead to Substitution of Labor for Capital?" Paper Commissioned by the Center for Futures Research, University of Southern California, 1975.

Bartell, Ted. "The Effects of the Energy Crisis on Attitudes and Lifestyles of Los Angeles Residents." Paper presented at the 69th Annual Meeting of the American Sociological Association, August 26-29, 1974.

Bell, Daniel. "The Corporation in the 1970s." *The Public Interest*, no. 24 (Summer 1971): 5-33.

Bengelsdorf, Irving S. "Drilling Would Destroy Unique Southland Coast." *Los Angeles Times*, October 13, 1974, part 6, p. 5.

Berg, Charles A. "Conservation in Industry." *Science*, 184, no. 4134 (April 18, 1974): 264-271.

Berndt, E. R., and Christensen, L.R. "Technology, Prices, and the Derived Demand for Energy." Discussion Paper 74-09, Vancouver: University of British Columbia, May, 1974.

_____. "The Translog Function and Substitution of Equipment, Structures, and Labor in U.S. Manufacturing, 1929-1968." *Journal of Econometrics*, 1, no. 1 (March 1973): 81-144.

Bezdek, Roger, and Hannon, Bruce. "Energy, Manpower, and the Highway Trust Fund." *Science*, 185 (August 23, 1974): 669-675.

Boretsky, Michael. "Trends in U.S. Technology: A Political Economist's View." *American Scientist*, 63 (January-February 1975): 70-82.

Boulding, Kenneth. "The Social System and the Energy Crisis." *Science*, 184, no. 4134 (April 19, 1974): 255-257.

Brand, David. "Global Report, New Tests Seen for U.S. Firms Abroad; Some Lands Try to Use Tidal Energy." *Wall Street Journal*, September 23, 1974, p. 6.

_____. "While U.S. Lags, France Rages Ahead With Its Nuclear Power Plant Design." *Wall Street Journal*, January 28, 1975, p. 36.

Bruce-Briggs, B. "Gasoline Prices and the Suburban Way of Life." *The Public Interest*, no. 37 (1974), pp. 131-136.

"The Burgeoning Benefits of a Lower Birth Rate." *Business Week*, no. 2310 (December 15, 1973): 41-42.

Carberry, James. "Oilmen, Blaming Price Controls, Pass Up Huge Amounts of Oil Left in Old Fields." *Wall Street Journal*, May 15, 1975, p. 34.

Carley, William M. "British Leyland Offers Textbook Case of Ills Afflicting U.K. Firms." *Wall Street Journal*, April 11, 1975, p. 1.

Carter, A. P. "Energy, Environment, and Economic Growth." *The Bell Journal of Economics and Management Science*, 5, no. 2, (Autumn 1974): 578-592.

Cates, William C. "Caught in the Tide, Energy Crisis Brings Setbacks and Windfall to Environmentalists." *Wall Street Journal*, January 2, 1974, p. 1.

_____. "Fact and Fantasy About Petrodol-

lars." *Wall Street Journal*, October 10, 1974, p. 16.

Chapman, Jeffrey, and Hunter, Hugh. "The Effect of Energy Availability On Industrial Structure." Paper commissioned by the Center for Futures Research, University of Southern California, 1975.

Chapman, P. R., Leach, G., and Slesser, M. "The Energy Cost of Fuels." *Energy Policy*, September 1974, pp. 231-43.

Christensen, L. R., Jorgenson, D. W., and Lau, L. J. "Conjugate Transcendental Logarithmic Production Frontiers." *Review of Economics and Statistics*, 55, no. 1 (February 1973): 28-45.

Cipolla, C. M. *The Economic History of World Population*. Baltimore: Penguin Books, 1962.

Clark, Wayne. "Energy Industry Capital Expenditures Forecast." Paper commissioned by the Center for Futures Research, University of Southern California, 1975.

"The Coming Glut of Energy." *The Economist*, 250, no. 6801 (January 5, 1974): 13.

Committee for Economic Development, Research and Policy Committee. *Achieving Energy Independence*. New York: Committee for Economic Development, 1974.

_____. *First World Symposium on Energy and Raw Materials: Summary of the Proceedings*. New York: Committee for Economic Development, 1974.

Compton, Dale W. "Energy Conversion and Storage Technology—The Sodium-Sulfur Battery." In *Energy Environment Productivity*, RAAN, National Science Foundation, 1974, pp. 25-26.

The Conference Board. *Energy Consumption in Manufacturing*. Summary Report, Volume I. New York: The Conference Board.

Cook, E. "Energy Sources for the Future." *The Futurist*, 6, no. 4 (1972): 142-150.

_____ . "The Flow of Energy in an Industrial Society." *Scientific American*, 225, no. 3 (September 1971): 134-144.

Daly, Herman E. *Toward a Steady State Economy*. San Francisco: W. H. Freeman, 1973.

Data Resources, Inc. "Problems and Prospects for the U.S. Economy: Data Resources Long-Term Projections, 1974-1985." May 1974.

Diamond, Robert A. ed. *Energy Crisis in America*, Washington, D.C.: International Standard Book, 1973.

Donovan, Robert J. "Mr. Blanding's Dream Home Is No More." *Los Angeles Times*, June 24, 1975, p. 5.

Dyckman, John W. "Speculations on Future Urban Form." Baltimore: Unpublished report, The Center for Metropolitan Planning and Research, The Johns Hopkins University, A-26.

Edison Electric Institute. *Questions and Answers About the Electric Utility Industry*. New York: Edison Electric Institute, 1973.

_____ . *Power and Progress*. New York: Edison Electric Institute, no. 67-54, 1967.

Ehrlich, Paul R., and Anne H. *The End of Affluence*. New York: Ballantine, 1974.

Elliot, Ward. "The Los Angeles Affliction: Suggestions For A Cure." *Public Interest*, no. 38 (Winter 1975): 119-128.

English, Morley. "The Long-Run Price of Energy Will Be Down." Paper commissioned by the Center for Futures Research, University of Southern California, 1975.

_____ . "Some Economic Concepts to Disturb the Engineer." *Engineering Economist*, 19, no. 3 (Spring 1974): 141-152.

"Enough Energy—If Resources Are Allocated Right." *Business Week*, no. 2333 (June 1, 1974): 50-60.

Environmental Education Group. *Public Interest Report—Solutions to the "Energy Crisis."* Adapted from a three-part public energy study, *Energy Options for Man*. Los Angeles: Environmental Education Group, 1973.

Environmental Protection Agency, Office of Research and Development. *Alternative Futures and Environmental Quality*. Washington, D.C.: Government Printing Office, 1973, p. 240.

Enzer, Selwyn. *Alternative Futures for California*. Report F-22 of the Center for Futures Research, University of Southern California, September 1975.

_____ . *Some Societal Impacts of Alternative Energy Policies*. Special Report WP-21. Menlo Park: Institute for the Future, January, 1975, p. 74.

Exeuctive Office of the President: Office of Management and Budget. *Social Indicators*. Washington: Government Printing Office, 1973.

Faucett, J., et al. *Data Development for the I-O Energy Model*. Final Report to the Energy Policy Project. Washington, D.C.: May 1973.

Federal Energy Administration. *Project Independence Report.* Washington: Government Printing Office, November 1974.

Fisher, John C. *Energy Crises in Perspective.* New York: John Wiley and Sons, 1974.

"The Food Crisis: Widespread Shortages Could Stir Hostilities, Pitting 'Have-Nots' against 'Haves.'" *Wall Street Journal*, October 3, 1974, p. 1.

Ford Foundation, Energy Policy Project. *A Time to Choose.* Cambridge: Ballinger, 1974.

_____. *Exploring Energy Choices: A Preliminary Report of the Ford Foundation's Energy Policy Project.* Washington, D.C.: The Ford Foundation, 1974.

Forsythe, Dall W. "An Energy-Scarce Society: The Politics and Possibilities." *Working Papers*, 2, no. 1 (Spring 1974): 3-11.

Frank, Helmut J. "Economic Strategy for Import-Export Controls on Energy Materials." *Science*, 184 (April 19, 1974): 313-316.

Friedlander, Gordon D. "Energy's Hazy Future." *IEEE Spectrum*, May 1975, pp. 32-40.

"Gallup Survey Finds 5% Drop In Use of Cars to Get to Work," *The New York Times*, February 16, 1975, p. 54.

Gannon, James P. "Future Fear: Is the Economy Sliding into Five Or Ten Years Of Stagnation, Unrest?" *Wall Street Journal*, May 15, 1975, p. 1.

Gapay, Les. "Weighing All the Energy Options." *Wall Street Journal*, December 13, 1974, p. 12.

Gaudion, Donald A. "Lack of Capital Perils

Industry's Future Growth." *Opinion*, Spring 1975, pp. 2-8.

Georgescu-Roegen, Nicholas. *The Entropy Law and Economic Process.* Cambridge: Harvard University Press, 1971.

Gordon, Richard L. "Mythology and Reality in Energy Policy." *Energy Policy*, 2, no. 3 (September 1974): 189-202.

Gould, J. P. "Adjustment Costs in the Theory of Investment of the Firm." *Review of Economic Studies*, vol. 35 (1968): 47-55.

Government Research Corporation. "Energy Policies and Problems." *National Journal Reports*, 5, no. 41 (October 13, 1973): 505-548.

Green, H. A. J. *Aggregation in Economic Analysis.* Princeton: Princeton University Press, 1964.

Griffin, J. M. "The Effects of Higher Prices on Electricity Consumption." *The Bell Journal of Economics and Management Science*, 5, no. 2 (Autumn 1974): pp. 515-539.

Hafele, Wolf. "A Systems Approach to Energy." *American Scientist*, 62 (July-August 1974): 438-447.

_____ and Manne, Alan S. "Strategies for a Transition from Fossil to Nuclear Fuels." The International Institute for Applied Systems Analysis, Schloss Laxenburg, Austria, June 1974.

Hammond, Allen L., Metz, William D., and Maugh, Thomas H., II. *Energy and The Future.* Chicago: R. R. Donnelley, 1973.

_____. "Zero Energy Growth: Ford Study Says It's Feasible." *Science*, 184 (April 12, 1974): 184.

Hartley, Fred L. *Oil Shale: Another Source*

of Oil for the United States. Address to *Oil Daily*'s Third Annual Synthetic Energy Forum. New York: Union Oil Company of California, 1974.

Heilbroner, Robert. *The Future as History.* New York: Harper, & Row, 1960.

Heller, Walter. "Taxes and the Capital Shortfall." *Wall Street Journal,* August 19, 1975.

Henderson, J., and Quandt, R. *Microeconomic Theory: A Mathematical Approach.* New York: McGraw-Hill, 1971.

Hieronymus, Bill. "With a Nod to History and Energy Crisis, Many Firms Renovate Their Old Buildings." *Wall Street Journal,* January 2, 1975, p. 4.

Hildebrandt, A. F., and Vant-Hull, L. L. "A Tower-top Focus Solar Energy Collector." *Mechanical Engineering,* September 1974, pp. 23-27.

Ho, Ping-Ti. "China's Resources Loom Large on World Stage." *Los Angeles Times,* October 13, 1974, Part 4, p. 1.

Hoffman, George A. "The Effects of Energy Price Escalations on Urban Transit Balance." *Transportation Research,* 8 (1974): 343-348.

_____. "Electric Bus Designs for Urban Transportation." *Transportation Research,* 6 (1972): 49-50.

_____. "Hydrogen-Rich Automotive Fuels: Future Cost and Supply Projections." *Proceedings of the Ninth Intersociety Energy Conversion Engineering Conference.* San Francisco: The American Society of Mechanical Engineers, 1974.

_____. "The U.S. Fuel Industry in the 21st Century." Paper Commissioned by the Center for Futures Research, University of Southern California, 1975.

Hudson, E. A., and Jorgenson, D. W. "U.S. Energy Policy and Economic Growth, 1975-2000." *The Bell Journal of Economics and Management Science,* 5, no. 2 (Autumn 1974): 461-514.

Ignatius, David. "The Capital Crisis: Crying Wolf on Wall Street." *The Washington Monthly,* 7, no. 9 (November 1975): 16-22.

Important for the Future, United Nations Institute for Training and Research, 1, no. 1 (September 1975): 17.

Industrial Research Institute, Inc. 1121 Technology Task Group. "Preliminary Report on the Delphi Forecasts on Energy and on Industrial Research." Unpublished report. New York, May 6, 1974.

Jacoby, Neil H. *Multi-National Oil.* New York: Macmillan, 1974.

Joint Committee on Atomic Energy. *Understanding the "National Energy Dilemma."* Houston: The Energy Institute, University of Houston and The Center for Strategic and International Studies, 1973.

Jorgenson, D. W., Berndt, E. R. Christensen, L. R., and Hudson, E. A. *U.S. Energy Resources and Economic Growth.* Final Report to the Ford Energy Policy Project. Washington, D.C., September 1973.

Jouvenad, Bertrand de. *The Art of Conjecture.* New York: Basic Books, 1967.

Kasper, Daniel, Kitch, Edmund, and Isaacson, Marc. "The Regulation of Taxicabs in Chicago." *The Journal of Law and Economics,* 14, no. 2 (1971).

Kennedy, Michael. "An Economic Model of the World Oil Market." *The Bell Journal of Economics and Management Science*, 5, no. 2 (1974): 540-577.

"Kissinger Lays Out His 'Floor Plan.' " *Time*, 105, no. 7 (February 17, 1975): 33-38.

Knowles, Ralph. "Urban Transformation: An Architect Looks at the Energy Problem." *Facets*, 1 (Spring 1975): 27-36.

Kristol, Irving. "The Credibility of Corporations." *Wall Street Journal*, January 17, 1974, p. 4.

Landaver, Jerry. "Not Too Long Ago, It Was Too Much Petroleum That Upset Firms." *Wall Street Journal*, March 27, 1974, p. 1.

Lansberg, Hans. "Low Cost, Abundant Energy: Paradise Lost?" *Science*, 184, no. 4134 (April 19, 1974): 247-253.

Lapp, Ralph E. "The Hard Energy Choices Ahead." *Wall Street Journal*, April 23, 1974, p. 26.

Lawler, Edward E., and Hackman, J. Richard. "Corporate Profits and Employee Satisfaction: Must They Be in Conflict?" *California Management Review*, 14, no. 1 (1971): 46-55.

Linden, A. "Energy Self-Sufficiency: A Look at the Future." *The Future Is Now*, Los Angeles: Council of Engineering and Scientific Proceedings Series, April 1975.

"Losing Power: How One Utility Sagged after Taking Giant Step." *Wall Street Journal*, October 8, 1974, p. 1.

MacMichael, David C. "Future Studies and Historical Method." Unpublished paper,

Stanford Research Institute, 1975.

Malinvaud, E. "Capital Accumulation and Efficient Allocation of Resources." *Econometrica*, 21, no. 2 (1953): 233-266.

Malley, Deborah. "Lawrence Klein and His Forecasting Machine." *Fortune*, 91, no. 3 (March 1975): 152-157.

Mancke, Richard B. *Performance of the Federal Energy Office*. National Energy Study 6. Washington, D.C.: American Enterprise Institute, 1975.

Mayer, Allen J. "All About the New Oil Money." *Newsweek*, 85, no. 7 (February 10, 1975): 58-63.

Mazur, Allen, and Rosa, Eugene. "Energy and Lifestyle." *Science*, 186 (November 15, 1974): 607-610.

Meadows, Dennis, Meadows, Donella, Randers, Jørgen, Behrens, William W. III. *Limits to Growth*, New York: Universe Books, 1972.

_____ . "Meadows: Curbing Growth." *Business Week*, no. 2380 (May 12, 1975): 58.

Melman, Seymour. *Our Depleted Society*. New York: Delta, 1965.

Mishan, E. J. "Ills, Bads, and Disamenities: The Wages of Growth." *Daedalus*, 102, no. 4 (1973): 253.

Mitchell, Edward J. *U.S. Energy Policy: A Primer*. Washington, D.C.: American Enterprise Institute for Public Policy Research, 1974.

MIT Energy Laboratory Policy Study Group. *Energy Self-Sufficiency: An Economic Evaluation*. National Energy Study

3. Washington, D.C.: American Enterprise Institute, 1974.

Mobil Corporation. "Toward a National Energy Policy." Advertisement in the *Wall Street Journal*, December 31, 1974, p. 7.

Mooz, W. E. "The Effect of Fuel Price Increases on Energy Intensiveness of Freight Transport." A report prepared under a grant from the National Science Foundation, Rand R-804-NSF, December, 1971.

_____ . "Energy Trends and Their Future Effects Upon Transportation." Rand Corporation, P-5046, July 1973.

"More Optimism, Less Resentment." *Time*, 105, no. 25 (June 16, 1975): 22.

Morton, Rogers. "New Sources of Energy Must Be Found at Home." *Los Angeles Times*, October 13, 1974, Part 6, p. 5.

Moultman, Jurgen. *Religion, Revolution and the Future*. Translated by M. Douglas Meeks. New York: Scribner's, 1969.

Nakamura, Leonard I. "Learning the Facts About Energy Needs." *The Conference Board Record*, 11, no. 8 (US ISSN 0010-5546), August 1974, pp. 5-7.

National Science Foundation. *Energy Environment Productivity*. Edited by Jay Holmes. *Proceedings of the First Symposium on RANN: Research Applied to National Needs*. Washington, D.C.: Government Printing Office, 1973.

Needham, James J. "The $650 Billion Gap." *Opinion*, published by the National Association of Manufacturers (Spring 1975), pp. 2-6.

Newman, Barry. "I Told You So, Environ-

mentalists Get Some New Ammunition from the Energy Crisis." *Wall Street Journal*, January 3, 1974, p. 1.

Nordhaus, William D. "Resources as a Constraint on Growth." New Haven: Cowles Foundation, paper no. 406, Yale University Press, 1974.

"The North Sea Bubble." *The Economist*. March 8, 1975, 254, no. 6863 (1975): 15-17.

O'Toole, James J. "Lordstown Three Years Later." *Business and Society Review*, no. 13 (Spring 1975): 66-71.

_____ . "The Reserve Army of the Underemployed." *Change*, May 1975, pp. 26-36.

_____ et al. *Work in America*. Report to HEW. Cambridge: MIT Press, 1973.

"Pay Now, Win Later." *Time*, 105, no. 3 (January 20, 1975): 69-70.

Pechman, Joseph A. *Federal Tax Policy*, New York: W. W. Norton, 1971.

_____ . "Record Capital Oil Outlays Aimed at Easing Shortages." *Oil and Gas Journal*, February 4, 1974.

_____ . "Companies' Spending Tops First Half Profits." *Oil and Gas Journal*, August 12, 1974.

Pierce, John R. "The Fuel Consumption of Automobiles." *Scientific American*, 232 (January 1975): 34-44.

Pimental, David, Hurd, L. E., Belotti, A. C., Foster, M. J., Oka, I. N., Sholes, R. J., and Whitman, R. J. "Food Production and the Energy Crisis." *Science*, 182 (November 2, 1973).

Pomrehn, Hugo Paul. *Technological Forecast of Energy Systems 1970-2020*. Unpublished Ph.D. thesis. University of Southern California, 1975.

Porter, Sylvia. "Why We Can't Afford Smog." *San Francisco Chronicle*, November 14, 1975, p. 62.

Quigg, Philip W. "Curbing Pollution from Ships" and "The World Food Shortage." *World Environmental Newsletter*, January 26, 1974, pp. 51-54.

_____ . "New Energy Sources: A Two-Part Summary of Their Prospects, Technology, and Environmental Impact." *World Environmental Newsletter*, February 9, 1974, pp. 47-50.

_____ . "New Energy Sources: Second in a Two-Part Series." *World Environmental Newsletter*, February 23, 1974, pp. 29-32.

"Rationing: Some Pros—But A Lot of Cons." *Time*, 105, no. 5 (February 3, 1975): 15-16.

Reed, T. B., and Lerner, R. M. "Methanol: A Versatile Fuel for Immediate Use." *Science*, 182 (December 28, 1973): 1299-1304.

Reich, Charles A. *The Greening of America*. New York: Random House, 1971.

Roberts, Richard W. "Energy Research: Scientists Seek to Ease the Pinch." *The Futurist*, 7, no. 1 (February 1973): 19-27.

Rose, Stanford. "The Far-Reaching Consequence of High Priced Oil." *Fortune*, 89, no. 3 (March 1974): 106-196.

Rueth, Nancy. "Energy: Alternatives And Risks." *ME News Roundup*, April 1974, pp. 88-89.

Ryan, Charles J. "Energy: The New First Estate." Edited by Anton B. Schmalz. In *Energy: Today's Choices, Tomorrow's Opportunities*. Washington, D.C.: World Future Society, 1974, pp. 129-138.

Samuelson, Robert J. "Can American Business Afford the Future?" *Los Angeles Times*, July 16, 1975, p. 5.

Schaltz, Joel. "Cosmic Economics." Edited by Anton B. Schmalz. In *Energy: Today's Choices, Tomorrow's Opportunities*. Washington, D.C.: World Future Society, 1974, pp. 281-289.

Schmalz, Anton B., ed. *Energy: Today's Choices, Tomorrow's Opportunities*. Washington, D.C.: World Future Society, 1974.

Schorr, Burt. "New Nuclear Regulating Agency to Face Hard Decisions on Atomic-Power Buildup." *Wall Street Journal*, February 3, 1975, p. 28.

Schumacher, E. F. *Small Is Beautiful: Economics as if People Mattered*. New York: Harper and Row, 1975.

Seaborg, Glenn T. "The Recycle Society." Edited by Anton B. Schmalz. In *Energy: Today's Choices, Tomorrow's Opportunities*. Washington, D.C.: World Future Society, 1974, pp. 20-26.

"Senate Unit Votes to Compel Auto Makers to Boost Gasoline Mileage 100% by 1985." *Wall Street Journal*, May 16, 1975, p. 32.

Shepard, Stephen B. "How Much Energy Does the U.S. Need?" *Business Week*, no. 2333 (June 1, 1974): 69-70.

Smil, Vaclav. "Energy and the Environment: Scenarios for 1985 and 2000." *The Futurist*, 7, no. 1 (February 1973): 4-13.

Stabler, Charles N. "Analysts Are Tracing Where Some Oil Funds Are Being Invested." *Wall Street Journal*, December 20, 1974, p. 1.

_____ . "Beyond Financial Transfer of Oil Money Lies The Trickier Problem of How It's Used." *Wall Street Journal*, September 30, 1974, p. 26.

Staff of the Mother Earth News. *Handbook of Homemade Power.* New York: Bantam Books, 1974.

Starr, Chauncy. "Energy and Power." *Scientific American*, 225, no. 3 (September 1971): 36-49.

Steinhart, John S. and Carol E. "Energy Use In the U.S. Food System." *Science*, 184 (April 19, 1974): 307-315.

Stobaugh, Robert. "The Hard Choices on Energy." *Wall Street Journal*, December 9, 1974, p. 22.

Stone, Tabor R. *Beyond the Automobile.* Englewood Cliffs, N.J.: Prentice-Hall, 1971.

Tanner, James C., and Ulman, Neil. "U.S. Firms That Own Aramco Agree to Yield 100% Control to Saudis." *Wall Street Journal*, December 6, 1974, p. 1.

Taylor, Stephen P. "A Financial Background for Project Independence." In *Project Independence: A Summary*, Federal Energy Administration, Washington, D.C., 1974.

Tavoulareas, William P. "Dissent of William P. Tavoulareas, President of Mobil Oil Corporation, to the final report of the Ford Foundation's Energy Policy Project." Comments on the Ford Foundation Energy Policy Project, *A Time To Choose.*

Teller, Edward. *Energy: A Plan for Action.* A report to the Energy Panel of the Commission on Critical Choices for Americans. New York: Critical Choices, 1975.

Train, Russell E. "The Long Term Value of the Energy Crisis." *The Futurist*, 7, no. 1 (February 1973): 14-18.

Treadway, A. B. "On Rational Entrepreneurial Behavior and the Demand for Investment." *Review of Economic Studies*, 36 (1969): 227-239.

Tussing, Arlon R. "Three Classes of Energy Resources." *Energy Policy*, September 1974, pp. 179-188.

Udall, Stewart, Conconi, Charles, and Osterhout, David. *The Energy Balloon.* New York: McGraw-Hill, 1974.

U.S. Congress. Senate. Committee on Interior and Insular Affairs. *Estimates and Analysis of Fuel Supply Outlook for 1974.* Washington, D.C.: U.S. 93rd Congress, 1st Session, serial no. 93-25 (92-60), Government Printing Office, 1973.

_____. *National Gas Policy Issues and Options.* Washington, D.C.: U.S. 93rd Congress, 1st Session, Serial No. 93-20 (92-55), Government Printing Office, 1973.

"U.S. Mustn't Rely on One Energy Source to Solve Long-Term Needs, Planners Say." *Wall Street Journal*, July 1, 1975, p. 2.

United States Trust Company of New York, Correspondent Investment Service. "A Discussion of the Energy Crisis." Unpublished report, 1973.

Uzawa, H. "Time Preference and the Penrose Effect in a Two-Class Model of Economic Growth." *Journal of Political Eco-*

nomy, 77, no. 4 (July/August 1969):
628-652.

Vincent, Phillip E. "What Are the Likely
Effects of Energy Availability on the Dis-
tributions of Income and Wealth?" Paper
Commissioned by the Center for Futures
Research, University of Southern Califor-
nia.

Watt, Kenneth E. *The Titanic Effect.* New
York: Dutton, 1974.

Wentorf, R. H., Jr., and Hanneman, R. E.
"Thermochemical Hydrogen Generation."
Science, 185 (July 26, 1974): 311-319.

"What America Thinks of Itself." *Newsweek*, 88, no. 24 (December 10, 1973): 48.

White, Lynn, Jr. "The Historical Roots of
Our Ecological Crisis." *Science*, 155 (March
10, 1967): 1203-1207.

_____. *Medieval Technology and Social
Change.* New York: Oxford University
Press, 1962.

Wigg, E. E. "Methanol as a Gasoline Ex-
tender: A Critique." *Science*, 186 (November 29, 1974): 785-790.

Wildhorn, Sorrell, et al. "How to Save Gasoline: Public Policy Alternatives for the
Automobile." Los Angeles: The Rand
Corporation Report R-1560-NSF, October
1974.

Winsche, W. E., Hoffman, K. C., and Sal-
zano, F. J. "Hydrogen: Its Future Role in
the Nation's Energy Economy." *Science*,
180 (June 29, 1973): 1325-1332.

Wong, William. "Easy Riding, Seattle's Free
Buses Revitalize Downtown Area." *Wall
Street Journal*, February 12, 1974, p. 28.

Yankelovich, Daniel. "The Upturn: How
Soon, How Strong?" *Time*, 105, no. 18
(May 5, 1975): 66-67.

Yergin, Daniel. "The Economic Political
Military." *The New York Times Magazine*,
February 16, 1975, p. 10.

Permissions

We gratefully acknowledge permission to reprint material from the following sources:

Roger Bezdek and Bruce Hannon, "Energy, Manpower and the Highway Trust Fund," *Science*, August 23, 1974. Copyright by the American Association for the Advancement of Science.

Kenneth Boulding, "The Social System and the Energy Crisis," *Science*, April 19, 1974. Copyright by the American Association for the Advancement of Science.

E. Cook, "Energy Sources for the Future," *The Futurist*, August 1972.

E. Cook," The Flow of Energy in an Industrial Society," *Scientific American*, September 1971.

Dall Forsythe, "An Energy-Scarce Society: The Politics and Possibilities," *Working Papers*, Spring 1974.

Hans Landsberg, "Low Cost Abundant Energy: Paradise Lost?" *Science*, April 19, 1974. Copyright by the American Association for the Advancement of Science.

Henry R. Linden, "Energy Self Sufficiency: A Look at the Future," Institute of Gas Technology, 1975.

Edward J. Mitchell, *U.S. Energy Policy: A Primer*, American Enterprise Institute, 1974.

E. F. Schumacher, *Small Is Beautiful: Economics As If People Mattered,* Harper and Row, 1975.

Chauncey Starr, "Energy and Power," *Scientific American*, September 1971.

John and Carol Steinhart, "Energy Use in the U.S. Food System," *Science*, April 19, 1974. Reprinted by permission of Duxbury Press.

Edward Teller, Hans Mark, and John S. Foster, *Power and Security*, D. C. Heath and Company, 1976.

Lynn White, *Medieval Technology and Social Change*, Oxford University Press.

Index